Go Create

Go Create

Rob Rawson

SAINT ANDREW PRESS
Edinburgh

First published in 2019 by
SAINT ANDREW PRESS
121 George Street
Edinburgh EH2 4YN

ISBN 978-0-71520-376-7

British Library Cataloguing in Publication Data

A catalogue record for this book is available from the British Library.

It is the publisher's policy to only use papers that are natural and recyclable and that have been manufactured from timber grown in renewable, properly managed forests. All of the manufacturing processes of the papers are expected to conform to the environmental regulations of the country of origin.

Typeset by Regent Typesetting Ltd

Printed and bound in the United Kingdom by
CPI Group (UK) Ltd

Contents

'How to' section

Acknowledgements

After a quiz on the radio, the presenter usually asks the contestant if they wish to say hello to anybody before they leave. The contestant then reels off a list of friends and colleagues and more often than not finishes with the phrase, 'and anyone else who knows me'. This helps to avoid the embarrassment of forgetting someone!

I could easily do the same by simply documenting 'anyone else who has helped me', but I am determined to be sincere and to include every single person who has helped me in any way to get from the proverbial blank canvas to the finished picture.

Staying with metaphors, my sister Catherine Hardcastle must take centre stage here. I am hugely grateful for all her help and guidance throughout the writing of this book. My colleague Diane Knowles has been meticulous with proofreading and together these two wonderful ladies have ensured a smooth flow to the text.

Thanks must go to the members of my review group: Peter Gardner, John Gibson and David Gray, all of whom, particularly in the early stages, kept me heading in the right direction.

Leaving metaphors behind, I owe a debt of gratitude to the following people who helped in the provision of research and material: Grace Gray, Lesley Hamilton-Messer, Tabi Harvey, Sue Hewitt, Catherine McIntosh, Kirsty McLellan, David Pitkeathly, Martin Poole, Neil Urquhart and Christine Smith.

I am also grateful for the support and encouragement of my colleagues in the Church of Scotland Mission and Discipleship team and in particular a former colleague, Iain Campbell, who helped to get this entire venture started.

Finally, a big thank you goes to my wife Lara and to my children Robert, David, Stephen and Eilidh who have had to endure my occasional bouts of grumpiness and impatience but who have also graciously cooperated with my photographic work, thus helping to produce a good number of illustrations for the book.

Acknowledgements for pictures

The following photos are gratefully acknowledged.

Page

15	Excellent graffiti sample, Iain Campbell
38, 39	Pictures of knitted poppies, Cameron Brooks (for both)
43	Advent Beach Hut, Beyond Church
48	Nativity Matchbox, Cumbrian Newspapers
80	Iain supervising a boy (graffiti art), C. L. Redford
81	Spraying through the stencil, C. L. Redford
82	Hanging up hardboards, C. L. Redford

All the other photos (including the pictures within the picture on page 82) are by the author, Rob Rawson.

Introduction

Thank you for choosing this book, which I think is unique! Try to imagine a simple Venn diagram (remember those from maths lessons?), where on one side you have a circle representing all kinds of arts-related books that are designed for church use – most often for children's groups. On the other side is a circle representing books on Christian mission and outreach. Now in your mind, see them interlocking – that's where this book sits. Based on the church calendar, it aims to encourage congregations to use arts-based projects not only to use their God-given talents but also to reach out and engage with their communities for the sake of the Gospel.

How can congregations be encouraged to do this?

There are two main responses I'd like to offer to that question. Firstly, I'd like to see congregations express faith and creativity through the arts and if that is to happen, then tasks need to be *made easy*. Many of us, given the right information and offered innovative, yet simple, ideas can easily engage (and enjoy!) all kinds of artistic projects.

Secondly, the accessibility of these ideas will, I sincerely hope, engage people who would never usually darken the doors of our churches. This book is written from a missional perspective and aims to encourage us to share those special moments in the Christian calendar with members of our communities, most of whom will know little or nothing about them. It is acknowledged that there are numerous community art projects that congregations may be heavily involved with, but this publication is more concerned with church-based projects that are centred on Christian celebrations and offer all kinds of opportunities for faith-sharing.

Therefore this book seeks to give church groups a raft of artistic yet easy to do ideas that enable them to involve their wider communities. In effect, this book is primarily an outreach resource that utilises the arts; not an arts book that incorporates outreach.

In summarising, it is simply something to encourage congregations to get creative and use that creativity to connect with their local communities. Once we've made that connection, then all sorts of opportunities can arise for us to share Jesus. That's the easy bit, isn't it?

I trust this book offers some fresh ideas, the realisation of people's potential, a good chunk of inspiration and, most importantly, an impetus for even greater outreach.

How to use this book

There is a very simple layout to this publication. It is not intended to be read from cover to cover (you can if you like, though) but is designed to be primarily a reference book. There are two main sections to the book. In the first section there are a number of suggested 'festivals' that provide the themes for undertaking projects. Each festival contains a selection of ideas relating to various art forms, along with suggested ways of how to engage the community through those ideas. If you have a Christian event coming up, such as Easter or Harvest, then you may prefer to go straight to the chapters relating to those.

In the second section of the book, most of the recommended art forms are outlined with clear instructions, along with details of the materials and tools required. In short, the second section is designed to encourage an attitude of 'can do' and to get you started.

There is no strict law to say that you have to do the arts projects that are suggested. You may choose an arts project relating to a different Christian event from the one you are planning for. Feel free to 'mix and match'! Furthermore, one of this book's aims is to encourage imaginative thinking from YOU! Ideas breed ideas and you may decide to flick through, look for a new concept, then simply take it and adapt it to suit your own situation.

Enjoy dipping in and out – or working through everything!

1

New Year

This is the day the Lord has made; let us rejoice and be glad in it.
Psalm 118:24

Introduction

Our conventional calendars start with January, named after the Roman god 'Janus', which means 'the gate'. In effect, January is the gateway to a new year ahead. We usually start the year with optimism and many of us make resolutions that are broken within a few days. Nevertheless, we may still re-dedicate ourselves to God and use the occasion to resolve to move forward in our personal faith journeys, or with others in our church, develop a missional culture, journey towards a vision, or aim to achieve specific objectives.

If the upcoming year is special for any reason, then this can provide a theme for activity. It could be something beyond the immediate community, such as an Olympic year (always a leap year, too), a royal celebration or jubilee and so on. Nearer to home, maybe something special is due to take place such as a significant anniversary (i.e. 25, 50, 100 years). A few years ago in a small Stirlingshire town, there was a weekend festival to commemorate the 50th anniversary of the closing of the local railway and its station. Although the demise of something is hardly a cause for celebration, the local community had rapidly grown and developed as a result of its railway heritage, so the anniversary provided a great excuse for model railway exhibits, all kinds of memorabilia and plenty of refreshments – mainly hosted, incidentally, on church premises.

Possible themes

So, faced with a twelve-month period ahead, and with all its potential, what possible themes can we apply to the start of the year? Here are just a few suggestions:

- New beginnings.
- Out with the old; in with the new.
- Gateways.
- Resolutions.
- 365 (366 in leap years) days to achieve/complete something.
- Starting out on a journey (where would we hope to be on 31 December?).
- Anniversaries and key events in the year ahead.
- Dedicating the year to the Lord (perhaps using the Lord's Prayer?).
- The year of the …

Artistic ideas around these suggested themes are endless. Let's have a look at a few.

So what could we get up to?

Broadcast with banners

The forthcoming year could be one of key significance for a congregation and so creating a banner to both celebrate and, in time, commemorate the year is ideal. The design is entirely dependent on whatever is to be celebrated, but to feature the year in large digits could be a good starting point. It is likely the banner may adorn the inside of the church building or the church hall – often a focal point for community activity, or can it go elsewhere?

Banner making is nothing new, of course. However, it is ideal for getting people around a table (or several tables) and working together on all kinds of tasks. While one person is cutting out a shape, someone else may be sewing material onto another piece of material. Yet another person may be gluing felt letters into position. This creates great opportunities for conversation. Engaging with our local communities requires building relationships and what better way to start that than having con-versations? A church in northeastern England holds a 'Crafternoon' every Monday, where people come together to knit, sew or try out other crafts while enjoying a chat

Some banners may have a theme for the year.

and a hot drink. Such groups could fundraise for a good cause, making the whole experience even more worthwhile.

I want to avoid stereotypes, but I sense readers thinking, 'Isn't this mainly for women?' While many of the banner makers I have met are indeed female, it can be a really satisfying experience for anyone. I'm a fairly typical 'bloke' who tends to shy away from needles (no, not the medical type – we *all* shy away from those!), but there's so much more involved in the process and I have found the designing, cutting, gluing and, yes, the chit-chat all very therapeutic. Quite often, it is those less frequently undertaken activities that prove to be so thoroughly enjoyable.

Late December to early January is, of course, a very cold period and so to gather in a well-heated church lounge or hall with friendly folk and a promise of a hot drink or two can provide a cosy prospect. This is therefore an ideal occasion to work on something creative *indoors*. If high numbers of people come through the doors, then a whole series of banners can be created. These may feature different aspects of the topic chosen. One church in central Scotland has four similarly designed banners that depict the name of the church, along with its mission statement, broken down into three key parts: *Knowing Christ better, Serving Christ together, Making Christ known to others.* These are hung from different pillars, strategically spaced apart so that the display becomes eye-catching as soon as you enter through the main doors.

Bear in mind that leaving banners hanging for year upon year will diminish their impact. They merely become part of the furniture and ignored. Worse still, they can get dusty and torn, which is hardly a good outcome for a sacred fixture. Remove them as soon as their relevance is felt to have passed by. Then you can hang new – and appreciated – banners in their place!

Time for a timeline

Often we begin a year by looking forward to a special anniversary but in doing so we reminisce and actually look backwards! A congregation about to celebrate a centenary, for example, will inevitably seek archive material on 'how it all began' and quite probably on a range of key events in the one hundred years since. A timeline is great fun to put together and can involve a considerable number of people from all corners of the local community.

A timeline need not necessarily revolve around the life of the congregation but can easily be concerned with, say, the history of the community itself, for example from the time of being granted a charter to becoming a royal burgh or since gaining city status. A parish model ensures that the local church has a key role in such histories and the further back in time we go, the more apparent the influence of the church becomes.

The timeline can take on many different forms for example a long 'frieze'. All kinds of artistic media may be used, but the overall effect is generally two-dimensional. It may not be particularly high, but in terms of length, it can be as long as you like! Having exhibition boards placed around a hall or the church sanctuary will allow for something of impressive proportions.

The possibilities are considerable. Photographs, documents, drawings and all manner of artefacts may be displayed. Different community groups could be invited to contribute to specific sections. Each will doubtless have archive material that should be of interest to those viewing the timeline.

Once completed, the timeline could be exhibited over a certain length of time, during which the church building or hall could be open to visitors. Members of the congregation can then provide a welcome, along with supplying a bounty of refreshments. Such hospitality should, no doubt, reflect well on the hosts.

As for the congregation's input, not only will there be church archive material to exhibit but also the task of constructing the timeline's 'back scene'. This may be made from all kinds of material, but perhaps the simplest material is lining paper, easily available from DIY stores. There are varying grades of thickness (naturally, the thicker paper will be more durable), but nearly all come in lengths of five or ten metres. The width or height is almost always 53.5cm (21 inches). Wallpaper may be used, but if it is bought new, it is usually much more expensive and quite often has an uneven surface, making writing on it far trickier.

A few years ago, an interesting alternative idea was adopted by a church near Glasgow. Instead of a physical timeline, an electronic version was created. There was still the opportunity for local people and groups to contribute, but material was then edited into a short, high quality video, accompanied by music and uploaded to the church's website.

Such a project could be launched with a dedication service, to which members of the community – particularly those who have contributed – can be specially invited and even encouraged to take part. (This last point will need to be dealt with sensitively. For example, requesting someone to say a prayer who happens to be a non-believer may be awkward.)

Simple souvenirs

Finally, why not give away fridge magnets? These little decorations are becoming ever more popular as souvenirs from all kinds of visitor attractions. They can also provide a good reminder of a particular event or project and a special anniversary year is no exception. A banner, as mentioned above, may incorporate a particular design and this could be copied onto a small card, laminated and then made into a fridge magnet by having an adhesive magnetic strip attached to the reverse. These flexible strips are usually available on a small roll from craft suppliers and are not expensive. Fridge magnets can be fun to create and as a 'freebie' publicity tool, may prove highly effective.

When celebrating any kind of anniversary, it is always good to ask questions like, 'What about the next hundred years?' or, 'Where do we believe God would want us to be in (number of years)?' People can then be encouraged to think of ideas and dream dreams (and maybe work together to bring those dreams to fruition).

For details on how to create banners and timelines, see Chapter 13.
For details on how to create fridge magnets, see Chapter 14.

2

St Valentine's Day

'Love the Lord your God with all your heart … love your neighbour as yourself.'
Mark 12:30–31

Introduction

Come February, we will inevitably think of romance when we hear the word 'valentine' and if we are in a relationship, we will also think of visiting a card shop! From a Christian perspective though, we can take the opportunity to look deeper into the subject of love and concentrate more on its spiritual aspects.

Valentine was a Christian priest in Rome during the time of Emperor Claudius the Second. The rule of Claudius was noted for its persecution of Christians and, despite it being illegal, Valentine risked his life to secretly conduct many Christian marriages. Eventually, he was caught and inevitably martyred. After initially being tortured, he was beheaded on 14 February although the precise year remains unclear. However, most historians seem to agree that his death occurred between 269 and 278 AD.

Perhaps because Valentine's ministry was by necessity a secretive one, the modern celebration has an element of mystery. Many of us will have sent cards to 'our valentine' without disclosing our name to add fun (and plenty of speculation!) to the occasion.

In modern times, the commercialisation of St Valentine's Day has meant we have lost sight of the Christian martyrdom aspect and allowed it to become more of a frivolous day of romance. However, the day can be a great opportunity for a congregation to reach out to its community with a loving message.

Possible themes

So, what angles can we take on this day of heart shapes, Cupid, arrows and pink, fluffy things?

- Love is …
- Love letters to/from God.
- Sacrificial love – Jesus' crucifixion, Valentine's martyrdom.
- Sending anonymous compliments to each other.
- The church saying it loves the community.

So what could we get up to?

Sending messages is very much at the heart of this celebration and so provides a massive opportunity for congregations to send messages to their neighbours, communities, or whomever they like!

Bonny bouquets

A banquet or posy of flowers can convey sentiments so much more than sending someone a card or letter. Providing small bouquets (sometimes also called 'lonely posies') is a fairly new and exciting idea that churches across Europe are adopting. It began in Belgium a few years ago simply as a way of bringing a smile to complete strangers. It involves a number of small bunches or 'posies' of flowers being strategically placed in public places. The bouquets have a small message label attached to them that may contain a piece of poetry or a Bible verse but invariably invite the 'finder' to take the flowers home as a gift.

Public places could range from a park bench or bus shelter to the public library or doctors' surgery (the latter two may need permission of course). The potential reach for these floral gifts is considerable. Left lying around the parish, with a simple message such as, *'With love from (name of church) to give to the one you love. If you have no one, then keep them for yourself, for God loves you.'* Messages can be much shorter, but the important elements to include are that the flowers are a gift from the church and that they are free to take away.

On a cautionary note, there are a few points to consider here. Firstly, flowers left in public places often signify a memorial to someone who has died. This is particularly evident when there has been a tragic accident on a stretch of road. Secondly, a person discovering the flowers may feel uncomfortable to be seen taking them away (even though this is their intended purpose). Where the flowers are left is therefore an important decision.

Also, mid-February is usually not the best time for availability of flowers, so it may be worth considering using seasonal varieties such as snowdrops or crocuses. Or create your own!

Arranging flowers is not a skill everyone has, so why not invite an experienced flower arranger to offer a demonstration of how to make a small bouquet or posy? A Valentine evening at, say, the church youth group could include such an activity. Young people could observe and then make one posy for their secret intended and another for the public 'giveaway'. Great fun!

A project title such as, 'I love (name of place)' may allow a number of activities, centred on the local church, which provide an opportunity for people to show their appreciation for their community in all sorts of ways. The bouquets may be just one aspect of a wider venture. Such a project could also include litter picking, tidying up public places, repairing a municipal clock, renovating a local landmark and so on.

Love letters

Love letters is a simple idea. Asking the local primary school children to write a poem is not uncommon, but why not invite them to write poems as love letters? These poems can be based on a theme of what the children love about their community or, indeed, about their local church. Running this idea as a competition and offering prizes, along with publishing the best ones in the church magazine, should encourage a good response. If someone from the church went into the school to explain the idea to the children and give examples, it would provide an extra opportunity for sharing the Gospel.

Putting across the simple message that God loves us can easily be included in such a project. An ideal way to do this would be by holding a special service at the church, within which the successful children can read out their winning entries. Their poems can then be complemented by other people reading poems and/or Bible readings that highlight God's love for all of us. For some children, it may be the first time they have attended a church service, but this kind of occasion should provide a positive experience for their initial visit.

Valentine video

Vox pops is an expression for impromptu, 'on the street' interviews. We see many of these sound bites on TV news items every day. Despite it being sometimes considered an invasion of privacy, a lot of people, when asked, are quite happy to offer a comment or opinion to a camera crew. Armed with an external microphone and a means to record, such as a camcorder, tablet or smartphone, you can capture a range of opinions from local people (or visitors) on the subject of what they love about the community and/or the church. An opening question could go along the lines of *'As we celebrate Valentine's Day, what would you say you love about this community?'* For those who may want to express an opinion but feel uncomfortable to speak, you could offer a card to hold up to the camera with the words, 'What I love in this community is …' and they can insert wording of their choice along the dotted line. The best items to use would be a dry-wipe marker pen and a small, reusable whiteboard. A4-sized whiteboards are easily obtainable from retailers. After each person has written their wording and has been filmed, you simply wipe away the wording and the card is clean and ready for its next user. The simplest solution is to print your initial wording on a piece of card and then laminate it.

Once you have as many opinions as you need, you can then produce a short video to show on a large screen in either the church hall or church building which may feature within a social occasion or special service. If advertised well, each person in the video may wish to go along and see themselves having their brief moment of fame! Of course, you need not restrict this to church property. Hiring out a local café or hotel room can prove a less intimidating environment for those with no church connection, and demonstrate that the church supports local business.

For details on how to produce good video productions, see Chapter 19.

Convivial confectionery

Some sweets can lend themselves very well to Valentine's Day. In the US there are *Candy Hearts*, while in the UK there are *Love Hearts* (other brands are available). The sweets contain varied little messages such as 'Be mine', 'Love me' and 'Ever yours'. Many of us will remember distributing them in the school playground and offering them to certain friends accordingly! The latest range of *Love Hearts* now includes emojis as well as romantic messages. The round, tablet-style sweets come in different colours with a message on one side, but both sides display a heart shape.

The range of colours can provide opportunities for artwork on a variety of scales. By using a specific colour among all the others, a mosaic of sweets could form a message such as, 'God loves you' or 'God is love'. Being relatively inexpensive, it is possible to buy several packets (arranged in tubes) and using greater numbers, create impressive images. Being sweets, it would be a shame not to eat any (!), so fixing them in place with jam or icing is recommended. You may either choose to use all the blank sides face up, or the sides with messages face up. Be aware, however, that some messages such as 'Hot lips' might not seem entirely appropriate!

Why not organise a competition to create an image with a love message to God? Each group or team can be given a certain number of *Love Hearts* tubes and invited to create a mosaic. It might be wise to permit entrants to submit a photograph of their creation so that, once finished, they can devour the sweets. Yet more sweets may be offered as prizes! How this is organised is entirely up to individual congregations, but the creative ideas are endless.

3

Lent

Create in me a pure heart, O God, and renew a steadfast spirit within me.
Psalm 51:10

Introduction

Lent is the time before Easter when we remember Jesus spending forty days in the wilderness, preparing for His ministry. He had just been baptised by John and had wandered into the harsh expanse of the Judean Desert to be alone, while praying and fasting. During this time, Satan repeatedly tempted Him, but Jesus successfully resisted, quoting scripture on each occasion. By the end of this period, He would have been physically weak but spiritually strong and well prepared for the challenges of the three years to follow.

Over centuries, Lent has inspired Christians to undergo fasting or some sort of privation in order to strengthen their faith. In recent times, this has often led to giving up chocolate (that includes me!), cakes, alcohol, etc. Invariably, such denial has involved forgoing more pleasurable aspects of food and drink instead of outright fasting and has not necessarily been to any purpose other than that of losing weight or improving will power rather than assisting in any spiritual development! This aspect of Lent has spread to those of little or no faith and the traditional feast before the fast – Shrove Tuesday – is fondly celebrated across the country as Pancake Day. So although the spiritual element of Lent is somewhat lost on people in the communities around us, there are, nevertheless, opportunities for us to connect with them.

Possible themes

There are two main angles here: Shrove Tuesday and the aspect of giving something up. Clearly, we want to introduce the spiritual meaning behind these, but initially we may need to dwell on the more secular but obvious 'connecting points'.

Shrove Tuesday

- All things involving pancakes (parties, races, tossing, etc.).
- Getting prepared for a challenge.
- Last minute clear out.

Giving something up

- Making sacrifices.
- Staying the course.
- Resisting temptation.
- Stickability/loyalty.

Period of spiritual training/renewal

- Prayer and/or meditation initiatives.

So what could we get up to?

Lent is preceded by the merriment of Shrove Tuesday and the day is mostly geared around eating pancakes, so that is where we will begin. Pancake mix can also make crepes and waffles. In truth, they are the same as pancakes but formed in a different shape. All forms are easy and quick to make and once out of the pan, can have any number of toppings added.

Pancake picture party

The consistency of pancake mix is such that it quickly solidifies as it hits a hot surface. If you carefully pour it out, it is possible to create all kinds of shapes, symbols, letters and numbers. Obviously, with a hot surface, this is an activity that requires risk assessment and appropriate supervision.

Pancake art is gradually increasing in popularity, especially in the USA. By gently squeezing a plastic bottle that has a long 'snout' (often used for sauces, mustard, etc.), it is easier to create detailed designs. As the pancake mix hits the pan, it solidifies quickly and starts to turn brown. Shading an image is done by squeezing out the mix for those parts of the image first, then squeezing out the lighter tones to fill in a few moments later. Obviously, the entire image must be 'joined up' or there will be no pancake! When the squeezing is over, simply flip over the pancake and see the image.

Pancake art is fun and simple images are easy to create.

For the start of Lent, why not have a pancake party and provide free pancakes along with the chance to win a 'best design' competition? There are varied ways this could be run. If young children are involved, decorating a pancake will be a safer option than shaping pancakes in the pan. Children love decorating with small sweets, cake decorations and so on. The possibilities for creativity are endless. The judging could be carried out by a chef from a local hotel or restaurant, or even a cook from the local school. Whoever is invited to judge would probably enjoy the celebrity status, too!

Tossing pancakes can be fun, but again, it will need careful thought about the risks. Hot pancakes flying up and down can be hazardous, particularly if space is limited and there are many people gathered around the activity. One possible solution is to use cold pancakes. Provided it is safe to run such an activity, it could be made competitive, with marks awarded for the number of flips in mid-air, or artistic merit in the style of the flips. Why not see if a local store could donate a new frying pan as the winning prize?

For details on pancake artistry, see Chapter 15.

Graffiti prayer wall

During Lent, many people seek ways to draw closer to God and this may involve a season of prayer. A number of congregations will open their church building during the season for anyone wishing to spend time in quiet prayer or reflection. Others run Lent courses, based on a variety of themes such as the Beatitudes or Jesus' resurrection. These initiatives sometimes involve people who are not regular churchgoers but who welcome an opportunity to explore prayer and issues of a spiritual nature.

Many people outside church will not consider praying (or even believe in a God who hears prayers), yet there are times when prayers are offered up by those who don't normally pray. There are often occasions, such as after a terrorist attack or during political upheaval, when people gather, perhaps around a memorial, to pray and reflect. There are certain issues that unite Christians and non-Christians, such as campaigning for social justice, promoting peace, supporting refugees and safeguarding the environment. Why not encourage people to pray about these in an artistic way?

We have all seen graffiti on walls, embankments, trains – just about anywhere! In most cases, graffiti is unsightly and is simply vandalism. However, it can also be incredibly artistic and eye-catching. As an artistic medium, its subversive nature often makes it highly popular with younger generations. Local churches can use the period of Lent to encourage both individuals and community groups to 'have their say' and offer up prayers in a radical way.

Combining graffiti and prayers may seem strange, but a prayer wall made up of graffiti-style images and statements can have a profound effect on those walking by and looking on. Those not inclined towards prayer may still be happy to 'voice' a prayer by painting phrases such as 'Lord, help us love our planet' or 'Please God, bring peace to (name of country)'. There is no need for much artistic skill, as letters and images can be represented by stencils, with the paint being sprayed over the

Using stencils in graffiti art makes it an inclusive activity.

stencils, using aerosols. The effects can be striking. On the other hand, some people with artistic flair may choose to paint their messages freehand.

There are, of course, a number of things to bear in mind when considering this kind of venture. Prayer walls could be literal walls, but unless on church property, it is rare to find a wall whose owner is willing for it to be 'decorated' in such a way! Canvas frames bolted together can be hung in a church building, church hall or even off-site in a local library or other public building. Furthermore, the potential for making mess is huge! Protecting property and clothing are obvious requirements, but face masks and plastic gloves should also be worn due to the nature of aerosols. Unless the artwork takes place outdoors, any indoor area must be well ventilated. Finally (and perhaps, obviously), if the displayed artwork is to remain outdoors, ensure the paints are weatherproof.

Powerful images are easily created through graffiti art.

For details on graffiti art, see Chapter 17.

4

Palm Sunday

'Blessed is he who comes in the name of the Lord!'
Matthew 21:9

Introduction

Holy Week starts with the celebration of Palm Sunday. This marks the occasion when Jesus rode into Jerusalem on a donkey and was cheered enthusiastically by crowds as He did so. While some laid palm leaves in front of Jesus (red carpet treatment), others waved palm leaves in the air, as was the tradition of welcoming a king.

Possible themes

- Jesus is king.
- Make way for Jesus.
- Humility (Jesus rode on a donkey).
- Welcome.
- Parade with flags or banners.

So what could we get up to?

There are many craft activities connected with palm leaves, but how do we connect with the wider community with this particular festival? In most of our communities, donkeys are hard to come by and spreading palm leaves on a street is fraught with potential problems, so the notion of a procession is perhaps not the most practical of ideas! Palm Sunday is very much about welcoming Jesus and on this occasion, a feasible community connection is with children at a local school.

A noisy school assembly

Most educational establishments are (thankfully) still open to acknowledging Christian festivals and a school assembly in which the Palm Sunday story is told allows for a good level of creativity. Making palm leaves is an obvious activity and there are numerous ways to produce striking-looking versions. Each class may adopt a different style and approach. The artwork can then be used in a role play of the 'triumphal entry', which may include a short drama – a script for which is provided at the end of this chapter. While church members could play the three key characters in the sketch, the children could be cast as disciples and members of the crowd. They would doubtless be delighted to have an excuse to make lots of noise and in the process may also capture a sense of what the original event felt like.

Palm parade

The whole notion of welcome should of course apply to churches at all times, but a specific welcome theme can lend itself very well to Palm Sunday. When people come into church, we welcome them in the name of Jesus. Why not welcome them like the crowd welcomed Jesus? Various community groups can be invited to create palms and these may be laid down on the floor of aisles or entranceways to the area where your congregation worships. So long as both the creators and the people entering for worship do not mind walking on them, the visual outcome can be striking. If your particular church property includes its own pathway or drive, such a welcome can be staged outside on an even bigger scale (weather permitting). To add to the effect, further branches can be waved during the service. Waving them during the singing would seem most appropriate, but a dramatised reading within which they can be waved, along with the shouting of certain phrases such as, 'Hosanna to the King!' or 'Blessed is he who comes in the name of the Lord!' would be another ideal moment.

Every year on Palm Sunday, a vast number of churches give out crosses made from palm leaves. These are often purchased from developing countries and in some cases from Christian-based, self-help projects. A congregation making its own palm crosses could have an adverse effect on the livelihoods of the current producers, so why not encourage existing trade by designing different types and sending the designs to the projects for production? Increasing the number of crosses ordered will obviously help the producers and so extending the outlay would be a good idea. Rather than restrict distribution to those attending the church service, try to be more 'inclusive' by giving them out on the street or leaving a good quantity on the counters of various shops. Always ensure that you have the relevant permission to do this and seek it sensitively.

Drama

A Palm Sunday story

'Tell this rabble to be quiet – we anticipate a riot!'

(The author gives permission for free copying of the script and free performance rights.)

Eliud and Josiah are two Pharisees (religious leaders) who are watching the crowds entering Jerusalem for the Jewish festival of Passover.

Eliud   Well, here they come! It's going to be a busy few days, Josiah.

Josiah   Indeed! They all seem to be behaving themselves, although I never trust those northerners from Galilee. They can get a bit rowdy if you ask me. I get no sleep with all their noise.

Eliud   So long as they pay high prices for the animal sacrifices, I won't be complaining. We need plenty of money for the temple repairs. Don't forget that leaky roof we had during the winter rains.

Josiah   Well that may be, but I'm still uncomfortable when they come down here. They've no manners! Besides, they've now got some prophet they're raving on about. Probably yet another crank!

Eliud   Don't look now, Josiah, but here come what look like Galileans. Hang on, they're starting to wave palm branches … and some are laying cloaks on the floor! What on earth is going on?

Jesus enters, surrounded by followers. Unless a suitable 'donkey' can be ridden, a fake donkey's head and neck can be used, while the followers closely surround and 'mask' Jesus in such a way that the body of the donkey could not be seen anyway. As he enters, the crowd shout …

Crowd	Hosanna! Hosanna! Blessed is he who comes in the name of the Lord! Hosanna to the Son of David! Welcome, Jesus!
Eliud	*(Having to shout.)* You were right about the noise, Josiah! But this seems excessive! Is this another of these prophets you were moaning about?
Josiah	*(Also having to shout.)* Yes, this is the latest hero of theirs. I believe he's called Jesus. What a commotion! We must stop this or the Romans will get stroppy. Hey you, Jesus! *(He struggles to get to him.)* Tell this rabble to be quiet!
Eliud	*(Also struggles to get to Jesus.)* Or we anticipate a riot! This lot are disturbing the peace! Order them to shut up!
Jesus	I'm afraid if you stopped the people praising God, then the very stones themselves will start shouting! Sorry! *(He continues riding.)*

The noise starts to die down as Jesus moves on and the crowds go with him.

Josiah	Well, what a cheek! *(Pause.)* This guy is going to be trouble, I'm sure.
Eliud	I have a strange feeling that there will be further commotion over the coming days. Just a feeling …
Josiah	He did seem to have something about him that I can't explain, but my word, he seems very popular.
Eliud	Give it a few days and we can turn the crowds against him. Hopefully, we can have him out of the way by next Sabbath.
Josiah	Next Sabbath? Oh yes, that's next Friday evening. Let's hope so!

(Exit.)

5

Good Friday

'Look, the Lamb of God who takes away the sin of the world!'
John 1:29

Introduction

Such a spiritually poignant day as Good Friday may not seem the ideal occasion to put on an arts project that can connect with non-Christians. The fact that it is a weekday would mean no 'regularity' of a Sunday service and not all countries celebrate it with a public holiday. However, events held in the evening can still prove successful, especially as a long holiday weekend is getting underway and a good number of people will be more flexible about their free time.

Good Friday commemorates the crucifixion of Jesus and through his death, it celebrates the subsequent 'payment' for all our sins. This massive, historical event is central to the Christian faith, without which we have no means of being made acceptable to God the Father.

Possible themes

- Salvation and/or redemption.
- Jesus pays the price.
- The sacrificial lamb.
- Jesus bridges the gap.
- God's love.

So what could we get up to?

The symbol of the cross (upon which Jesus suffered and died) is instantly recognisable as the main image to represent Christianity – just as much as the Star of David is associated with Judaism, or the star and crescent moon with Islam. So many artistic ideas have, over centuries, been centred on the shape of the cross and our first project is based along those lines.

A cross in bloom

Of all the artistic projects in this book, this is unique in that it needs considerable forward planning. In fact, the project itself comes a few months before Good Friday and depending on nature's timing, may not actually coincide with the day itself!

Allow me to explain. A few years ago, I learned of a Christian youth group in southeast England who had been granted permission to plant a vast number of daffodil bulbs on the embankment of a major road. The group planted the bulbs in such a way that the following spring, as the daffodils came into bloom, a large, yellow – and very conspicuous – shape of a cross adorned the embankment. Passing motorists would have been given a highly visual reminder of the Easter message!

So much civic pride manifests itself in floral displays. Planting flowers that make up images and words can be found in villages, towns and cities just about anywhere. A church can easily collaborate with its local authorities or civic societies to help create colourful and attractive displays, so offering to help create an image that reflects a key festival such as Easter would not be unreasonable. Easter usually coincides with daffodils coming into bloom, but as springtime can arrive at differing times and the Easter weekend also moves from year to year, such an activity cannot guarantee perfect timing. Daffodils usually bloom in between the crocuses that come earlier and the tulips that come later, so why not plant a variety of flowers in order to both reinforce the message and ensure Good Friday coincides with a display of one sort or another?

As an outdoor activity that can involve a good number of people, it is certainly worthy of consideration, particularly as it provides opportunities for all kinds of conversations. Hopefully, many of those conversations will involve the meaning of the cross and the sharing of faith.

Passion plays

Passion plays have been known to be performed on a grand scale with a huge cast, impressive scenery and backed with a musical score. There is an historical reason for this. Passion plays sprung up across Europe in the Middle Ages when local churches had by far the most influence on their communities. In an age of high illiteracy, the churches encouraged their local town guilds to come together and help educate people by retelling the Easter events through a series of dramatic scenes staged on wagons around the town square. Each guild would contribute according to their profession. Weavers would provide costumes; woodcutters would provide the crosses, blacksmiths the Roman weaponry and so on. Such local collaboration is still feasible today through various civic groups, although the potential scale for many ventures may be considerably less, especially in smaller communities. The whole idea of passion plays may put many off, simply because of the expectation that it would need to be staged in an expansive way.

So can most of us stage anything at all? Yes, of course! There are so many ways to perform drama that it makes the art form far more inclusive than many would think. Let us have a look at some options ...

The first consideration is whether to stage outside or inside. The weather in Britain is always unpredictable, so ensuring shelter both for performers and onlookers is preferable. Unless an awning or temporary roof is available for performing out-side, an indoor production is probably going to be the best option. That doesn't necessarily mean one venue either. Different scenes (the betrayal, trial, crucifixion, etc.) may be staged inside different buildings around the village or town. There is no limit to one's imagination here. Certain rooms or halls may lend themselves well to a particular scene. Often, church sanctuaries have a raised platform at the front, along with a high-backed chair. This would be ideal for the trial scene, with Pontius Pilate seated in the chair.

Using single indoor venues is perhaps more in line with most congregations' capabilities. A series of tableaux may be arranged around a large hall or, depending on space, around the church sanctuary.

Another option is whether to have a large or small cast of actors. Most congregations will find the latter fits more within their capabilities and the old saying 'small is beautiful' may well be the case. Having one actor narrating and others miming to the narration is a simple method, but visually it can be very effective and – this will be good news to many – it requires no learning of lines!

How you stage your play brings up yet more options. It also presents plenty of opportunities for outside involvement. The creating or painting of scenery, making costumes and providing props are all ways to get people involved. Many high schools include activity days in their curriculum, as well as looking to provide work experience for their older students. The range of handiwork that may be needed for your play can, with appropriate supervision and legal checks, help to meet such educational requirements.

If you choose to perform the play within church grounds or simply within the church building, there may be a tendency to think that fewer unchurched people will want to come along. However, having different parts of the community involved in creating the production (and even taking part in the performance) always attracts a wider audience. This especially applies to friends and relatives of those 'stars' in the cast.

For more information on performing drama, see Chapter 18.

6

Easter

'He is not here; he has risen, just as he said. Come and see the place where he lay.'
Matthew 28:6a

Introduction

Easter is such a significant festival in the Christian calendar. Without its events, the whole of Christianity would simply not exist. In order for everyone to obtain forgiveness and live a new life in Christ, Good Friday and Easter Day had to happen. In the Biblical narrative, we read the angel's proclamation in Luke's account: *'He is not here; he has risen! Remember how he told you in Galilee: "The Son of Man must be delivered into the hands of sinful men, be crucified and on the third day be raised again." Then they remembered his words.'*

Despite its huge significance as a Christian festival, much of Easter's traditions have their roots in pagan practices. Eggs were considered as both symbols of fertility and as representing the rebirth of the land. Decorating them to present as gifts at springtime was an ancient custom. The tradition of egg-rolling goes back hundreds of years but is considered to have its roots in the Christian Easter. The hare is thought to be a symbol of the pre-Christian Saxon goddess Eostre, whose feast took place at the spring equinox. It is easy to see the connection with the present-day Easter Bunny. Sadly, much of the Christian aspect of Easter has been lost on modern society, yet the ancient customs remain highly relevant and very popular!

Possible themes

- New life.
- The empty tomb.

- Jesus conquers death.
- Rebirth and regeneration.

So what could we get up to?

It is inevitable, especially among younger people, that towards Easter, our minds will turn to eggs. These eggs will, no doubt, be of the chocolate variety, but I would like us to think of natural hens' eggs which can provide us with artistic opportunities.

Eggstravaganza!

Generally speaking, eggs are easy to obtain and inexpensive to buy. As a result, an egg-painting activity is relatively easy to organise. Preparation will mainly consist of hard-boiling lots of eggs and obtaining paints, brushes and cleaning materials. While this is an obvious Sunday School or Messy Church pastime, how can we use it to engage with the wider community? Having a sign outside a church hall saying 'Egg-painting inside!' is probably not going to pull in any great crowds from the street, so a bolder approach is necessary. Many congregations are learning that they cannot expect the community to come to them anymore but that they now have to go to the community. This activity therefore needs to be held 'off site'. One obvious suggestion would be to use a market stall or table in a local square or a pedestrian-ised street (having obtained the relevant permission from local authorities) and simply offer the activity free of charge to passers-by. Making it free will naturally prove popular but also sends out a message that the local church is not always after money! It would be helpful to provide folding chairs so people can relax as they paint, along with a canopy or awning in case the weather is poor. Any artists among the congregation could paint a number of eggs in advance and these could then be placed on display to inspire the visitors. It is important that you make it obvious who you are and, if possible, that the designs are geared around the resurrection story. You can talk about the Easter story as people sit and paint, but if a design of a bunny or spring flowers ends up on an egg, don't feel disappointed! You have still shown the church to be actively engaging with people and offering an enjoyable and creative activity. It goes without saying that the visitors can keep the eggs they have painted, but as the paint will need to dry, you could offer to store them for a short time while the visitors continue their shopping. (It would be wise to begin conversations with explaining this, just in case visitors do not have the time to return to your stall.)

Alternative venues may be a school (you could run a competition for the best design), a leisure centre, library or even a pub. In all these cases, it is best to offer the activity for free and for participants to keep their eggs.

Empty tomb egg cups

The policy of offering free services or gifts cannot be stressed enough. We have all used fairs, fun days and concerts to raise money, so to offer something for free can challenge people's perceptions. In so doing, we say that we value those in our communities by providing something for them at our own expense and don't necessarily want to empty their wallets!

So why not give away some chocolate Easter eggs? As above, there are many public places where we can hand out free eggs (mainly of the smaller variety that are individually wrapped), but the artistic 'twist' is to give them away along with an egg cup that is designed as an empty tomb. The easiest way of doing this is to purchase packets of clear plastic 'shot glasses'. These are often used for dispensing medicine, partaking in Holy Communion or even (as the name suggests) for drinking something stronger! They usually come in packs of ten, twenty or more and are very inexpensive.

Using poster paints, place glasses upside down and paint the entire glass in grey, to represent stone. Then use black paint to create a small tomb entrance at the foot of the glass. Next to this, using a lighter shade of grey, paint a round stone that is slightly bigger than the entrance. This signifies the rolling away of the stone from the entrance. Using some green paint, you can then add bits of grass or foliage around the foot of the glass to add a touch more authenticity. Once dry, use some white paint to write 'He is risen!' on the other side of the glass. When the whole glass is dry, you can invert it and place a small chocolate egg inside, thus creating an egg cup. When you give the egg away, you can mention that the egg cup comes free as well and is to be kept as a reminder of the Easter story. At the same time you may wish to give out an invitation to an Easter service.

As the paints dry on the plastic, they may lose some of their brightness and intensity, so you may prefer to use small coloured stickers to represent the tomb entrance and the greenery. The actual painting and decorating of the egg cups is entirely up to people's imagination and can prove a very enjoyable activity, especially to younger people.

All this painting begs the question, 'What are the best paints to use?' Virtually any type of paint will work on egg shells and the plastic glasses, but poster paints tend to be inexpensive, easy to clean if spilt and relatively quick to dry. Try to use artists' brushes, rather than cheap ones, as their stiffness and pointy ends allow for more precision. This especially applies for writing any words.

For further information on the egg initiatives, see Chapter 14.

7

Pentecost

'Then Peter said to them, "Repent and be baptised, every one of you, in the name of Jesus Christ for the forgiveness of sins and you shall receive the gift of the Holy Spirit."'
Acts 2:38

Introduction

Pentecost (also known as 'Whitsuntide') comes towards the end of May and commemorates the time in Jerusalem when the apostles, having witnessed Jesus ascend to Heaven, received the Holy Spirit. With all the commotion of the apostles being able to speak in other languages, people started to gather around. Peter, emboldened by the Holy Spirit, addressed the crowd and delivered a powerful Gospel message, which had a profound effect. The crowd responded positively by asking Peter what they should do and he told them to repent, come to faith in Jesus and they, like him, will receive the Holy Spirit. The account of this in Acts 2 goes on to say that some three thousand were added to the fellowship that day. I wonder how many congregations would love to see that kind of growth today! In effect, this defining moment in the history of Christianity has become generally regarded as the birth of the global Church.

Possible themes

- The Holy Spirit.
- The enabling/helping of the Spirit.
- Power from above.
- Birthday of the Church.

So what could we get up to?

The last bullet point above provides a straightforward theme for a whole range of activities. Birthdays often include parties and within those parties are found a good number of artistic opportunities. Parties usually include decorations, food and fun activities or games. When I was a little boy, my birthday parties included all guests having to perform a 'party piece', for which they would receive a small prize and a piece of cake to take home. That tradition is perhaps more outdated today, but the term 'party piece' has not entirely disappeared from our vocabulary and may provide an opening for some artistic talents to shine.

Performing party pieces

It is not too difficult to organise a party in, say, the church hall. Usually a small group of volunteers will get together to outline tasks and agree on who will do what task. This can range from booking the date and venue to baking and/or decorating a big birthday cake. For a birthday party for the church (to be held as near as possible to Pentecost Sunday), let us assume that all the foundational work is complete so we can concern ourselves with who we invite and what may take place at the party.

It should be a fun-filled event, so inviting people from outside the congregation should be a lot easier than perhaps inviting the same people to a regular Sunday service. The nature of the party may determine the people you invite. If it is to be the type that includes run-around games, jelly and ice cream and spot-prizes, then children will be your 'target audience'. On the other hand, hot food, 'parlour games' and maybe a quiz will appeal more to older people. You may, of course, try an all-age approach by featuring a mixture of both. *How* you invite is a key ingredient to success or failure. If you put a poster up on a church noticeboard or highlight it on a church website, do not be surprised if interest ranges from modest to downright poor. In our high-tech age, word-of-mouth is still highly effective. By chatting with our unchurched friends, we can invite a lot of people – especially if the event is free. After all, it would not be much of an invitation if paying was part of the deal!

A furthering of the invitation (and this may well influence who is to be invited) would be to ask the person(s) concerned if they would like to perform a party piece. A lot of our friends have certain talents and in a number of cases, some hidden talents, too. TV shows that seek to discover new talent are commonplace, so why not offer a 'talent show' that may even include a panel of judges and a prize for the winner? On a more informal level, we may term it as an 'open mic' time. Singing, juggling, conjuring, telling jokes (be careful about material here!), dancing and reciting poetry are just a few ideas.

Crucially, however, we will want to get across what the birthday party is all about and so it would be helpful at some point to include a message, such as a brief epilogue or even a short drama sketch, which outlines the meaning of Pentecost and appropriately describes the person of the Holy Spirit. We are keen to introduce people to Jesus, so events like these will help to build up relationships and allow for discussion as we travel home from the party or meet for a coffee on a later occasion.

One such drama sketch, written by yours truly, is included at the end of this chapter and only requires two actors. It is freely available to copy and perform.

A birthday 'bake off'

A lot of our current TV programmes involve individuals taking part in cookery or baking competitions. They are very popular and have spawned numerous localised versions. Having a birthday cake bake off provides an ideal opportunity to invite members of the community to try their hand at baking a birthday cake for the local church. If you have a baker in your community, invite him or her to be the judge (but not to compete, as they will probably have a distinct advantage!).

At the aforementioned party, once the judging is over, the entrants' cakes can be eaten as part of the food on offer. The judging will give the birthday party a 'high point' in the proceedings and present a good story and photographic opportunity for the local press.

Finishing touches

Designing posters, banners and creating all kinds of decorations – even creating a winner's sash for 'best cake baker' or 'best party piece performer' – can help get a lot of people involved in making a birthday party creative and memorable. The more effort we put into the occasion and the more we add sparkle to it, the more special our guests will feel. What a witness that would be!

Drama

Birthday blues!

(The author gives permission for free copying of the script and free performance rights.)

Bill and Bob are a couple of retired, old 'blokes' who enjoy nothing better than sharing a park bench, reading their newspapers and talking about everything and anything. They are Christians but perhaps a little 'on the fringe' when it comes to their faith! They are portrayed as 'trans-Pennine' but could be from anywhere in Britain and thus possess the appropriate local accent.

Bob is seated on the bench, lost in thought, staring ahead. Enter Bill.

Bill How do, Bob! By 'eck, you look a bit down in the dumps! Cheer up, it might never happen!

(As he sits, he gives Bob a friendly nudge and chuckles. Bob isn't particularly moved!)

Bob Oh don't say that! You see, I *do* want it to happen, but it's six months away!

Bill *(Puzzled.)* What is?

Bob My birthday! I couldn't be further away from my last birthday or my next one. As you know, it's in November – the opposite time of year – and that's so depressing.

Bill Blimey, Bob, you sound like a wee kid!

Bob No, it's just that my wife promised me a brand-new lawn mower for my birthday, but I could do with it right now, as our grass looks like a bloomin' meadow. Trouble is, when I do finally get it, it'll almost be winter!

Bill	Oh, I see.
	(Tries to be upbeat.) Still, it's a nice time of year, this!
	(Pause.) Besides, it's birthday time at the church, so I hear. Starting tonight, we're having a party!
Bob	Why, whose birthday is it? Is it old Edith Boothroyd? She *must* be a hundred by now!
Bill	No, it's ours! The church itself! When you slipped out to sneak off to the football last week, you missed the announcement. This week is 'Penta-gon' or something. *(Thinks hard.)* No, not Pentagon … I mean … er … Pent … Pentateuch?
Bob	Pension? Pentathlon? Penthouse?
Bill	No, no … *(Suddenly remembers.)* Pentecost! That's it! We're celebrating the church's birth.
Bob	I thought our church began in January, back in 1879?
Bill	No, not this church here. The whole church – when folks first came together to worship as followers of Jesus. This weekend, we're having a bit of a knees-up!
Bob	Sounds great, but I thought the main church birthday was Christmas – when Jesus was born. What's this other one you're banging on about?
Bill	It's when that wind and fire thing happened – when the Holy Spirit came. Quite a moment!
Bob	*(Cheers up.)* Oh yes! By gum, that caused a bit of a stir at the time but loads of folk joined up!
Bill	Exactly! So why don't *you* come and *join us* tonight and celebrate?
Bob	Aye, forget the bloomin' lawn mower! *(Gets up.)* Let's go!

(Both exit, singing 'Happy Birthday'.)

8

Harvest

'He makes grass grow for the cattle, and plants for man to cultivate – bringing forth food from the earth: wine that gladdens the heart of man, oil to make his face shine, and bread that sustains his heart.'
Psalm 104:14–15

Introduction

Harvest Festival is a key event in the Christian calendar, especially so in more rural areas. It is a time to give thanks for all that God provides and sustains us with. This autumnal anniversary goes right back to early Old Testament times when God's people celebrated 'Sukkot' or the 'festival of booths' or 'shelters'. This was a time when the harvest was gathered in and farmers made shelters for themselves while working hard out in the fields. Today, many Jews still construct temporary booths and both eat and sleep in them over a week-long festival.

Perhaps the most abiding memory for Christians from numerous Harvest Festivals is singing the hymn, 'We plough the fields and scatter'. Yes, our farmers put in some very hard work throughout the year, but the key line in the first verse is, 'but it is fed and watered by God's almighty hand.' We recognise that every single thing we have ultimately comes from our Creator and Sustainer God.

Possible themes

- Thanksgiving.
- The land.
- Food, especially fruit, vegetables and bread.
- Fair trade issues.
- Sowing and reaping.

So what could we get up to?

Saying thank you to God can be a general theme that may be particularly high-lighted at harvest time. How we say it can be done in a number of creative ways, but using the theme of agricultural produce can be great fun!

Say it with food!

Many congregations across the world work hard to put on a beautiful harvest display in their church sanctuaries. Flowers, fruit, vegetables and bread are carefully arranged to provide an impressive, worshipful reminder of God's provision at Harvest Festival. Those attending the main harvest service also bring offerings of food to add to the display then after the service the food is distributed to those in the community in most need of it. These days, however, fewer and fewer people from our communities come to these services to witness and appreciate such scenes.

Over recent years, local food banks have sprung up and grown in numerous localities. Congregations have been key players in their evolution. It has been both a sad and a joyous development; sad because we have a society that has created such poverty that the basic need of daily food cannot be met for so many people, yet joyous in seeing how communities – and in particular, local congregations – have responded. While Christians support these initiatives to demonstrate Christ's love, the humanitarian aspect of food banks will attract many non-Christians and so many current ventures are jointly run by churches and other local agencies. This presents a good opportunity for us.

Creating an eye-catching display of food items in a public place or in prominent church grounds which acknowledges God's provision, yet supports fairer distribution of that provision (such as your local food bank), can offer a great opportunity for cross-community collaboration. The end result may well attract a lot of positive attention and generate goodwill between your church and various community groups.

The nature of the display depends on location. An outdoor grassy bank is ideal to spell out a message, but a flat lawn will only allow a view from above. Shop windows present good opportunities but may lack the space for an attention-grabbing message. Indoor displays in civic halls, schools or even hospitals can prove very effective by reaching a much wider audience and offer the opportunity to have people on hand to speak to 'visitors' and give out publicity material.

The display can consist of words spelt out by arranging food items accordingly. A simple phrase such as 'God provides – let us do likewise' or 'God gives – let us share', should help those seeing it to think deeper about harvest and its meaning.

Food items that will survive the timescale of your display may involve cans of vegetables or fruit, boxes of cereal, packets of dried food (pasta, lentils, beans, etc.), bottles of sauce, tins of biscuits and packets of cream crackers or oatcakes. The list could go on, but the key point is that items need to be able to be kept for a reasonable length of time and as they are sealed, they can be handled and arranged without any risk to hygiene.

Schoolchildren will particularly enjoy designing and laying out these messages. If it is impractical to use food items, then cutting out images of food from magazines or unwanted cookery books and laminating them is a simple alternative. Laminating helps preserve the cut-out images and allows for sticking an adhesive on the back for mounting.

A presentable present!

Once food has been collected up and is ready for distribution to those needing it, why not add a touch of God's love by presenting it in an attractive basket, box or bag? So many individuals in our congregations can knit and a good number can use all sorts of materials in a creative way. Depending on the weight and size of the food (cans and jars can be heavy), you may wish to knit small bags for fruit and vegetables or make a wooden 'tool box' with a carry handle for a few cans of beans or peas. Some containers may be specifically designed for certain foods. A cylindrical container for example, would be ideal for packets of breadsticks or a few bananas. If built to last, these containers may then serve the recipients for future shopping or for trips to their food banks. These should be lovingly decorated and a Biblical message added.

There is no limit to our imagination and meeting up to work together on making various containers can attract many from outside the congregation. Opportunities for conversation and relationship-building will naturally present themselves.

Each autumn, many youngsters get involved in shoebox appeals, where old shoeboxes are filled with small Christmas gifts such as toys and useful items such as a (new!) toothbrush or comb. They are then decorated and gift-wrapped and sent to less fortunate children in developing countries. Using shoeboxes is ideal for lighter food items and easy for children to decorate, especially if they are experienced with the appeals. You may wish to co-ordinate a joint appeal with existing projects, but you will need access to a lot of shoeboxes!

For details on how to create simple baskets, see Chapter 14.

9

Remembrance

'Greater love has no-one than this, that he lay down his life for his friends.'
John 15:13

Introduction

Remembrance Sunday in the United Kingdom always falls on the nearest Sunday to 11 November. That was the date in 1918, when at 11 o' clock in the morning all guns fell silent, as the Armistice to end the Great War came into force. Each year at this time we pause to remember the sacrifice of those in our armed services who fell, not only in that terrible conflict but also in World War Two, the Korean War and more recent conflicts such as the Falklands War and those fought in Iraq and Afghanistan. We give thanks for the sacrifice they made to ensure the freedoms we now enjoy and so easily take for granted.

Large-scale projects produce striking displays for remembrance. (See detail opposite.)

Parish churches are usually much fuller on Remembrance Sunday, especially as many veterans and members of uniformed organisations also attend to parade their colours. Some members of congregations have been known to feel almost 'put out' that their Sunday services have been taken over and ask questions such as, 'Where are they on Sundays for the rest of the year?' I am not suggesting such people are unsupportive but that perhaps they feel that such ceremonies should be separately organised. On the other hand, the services can be seen as an ideal missional opportunity when so many unchurched people join with us for a time of worship, albeit in a different form from more regular Sunday worship.

So much activity happens around these services. Poppies are sold to raise funds for families of the dead and injured, acts of remembrance take place in public places and a special televised act of remembrance, attended by royalty, takes place in the Royal Albert Hall on the preceding Saturday evening. Poppies begin to appear from late October and so remembrance is very much in the public consciousness for around four weeks each year. This timeframe provides a generous 'window of opportunity' for artistic projects.

Detail of knitted poppies at St Andrew's High Church in East Lothian (opposite).

Possible themes

- Love and sacrifice.
- Gratitude.
- Courage.
- Service.
- Reflection.
- Caring for the afflicted.
- Just causes.

So what could we get up to?

Remembrance is a time of heightened feelings and emotions, so we will need to approach projects with a considerable degree of sensitivity. It is likely we will have close historical connections with some who have fought (and died) and may come into contact with others who have similar past or even current connections. We can still enjoy ourselves, but the art forms we use and the ideas we may come up with must always be respectful.

Poppies on parade

One of the key features of remembrance is the wearing of imitation poppies to show our support for those affected by the sacrifice of their loved ones and also to demonstrate our desire not to forget this sacrifice. The scale of loss, particularly in the two world wars, can never be fully appreciated, but huge displays of thousands of poppies can have a striking visual effect. A church in eastern Scotland recently 'planted' four thousand knitted or crocheted poppies in their garden that had been carefully created by just twelve members of its craft group. The garden backed on to the main street of their town, where many passers-by could see the stunning effect of the lawns having virtually turned from green to red. Just a bit further east, another church knitted or crocheted a staggering six thousand poppies to create a huge display that contained the words, 'Lest we forget'.

Many people in our communities can knit or crochet and will also want to support a project along these lines. Having the display outside your church building will attract much welcome attention and make the statement that the congregation stands with those in the community who have suffered loss either in past or current generations. To create something on a vast scale requires much forward planning and you will need to recruit a good number of knitters. The aforementioned craft group took nine months, so you will need to allow plenty of time for large scale numbers.

Getting together to work on a project can, as always, create lots of conversations and in this particular case, encourages all to keep up with a good pace of production!

Ideas for a display could range from creating phrases like, 'We will remember them' to forming shapes or images, such as that of a cross or of a soldier with head bowed.

Mini memorials

An ideal artistic project for children would be to create their own miniature memorials. Salt dough is good material to create a stone effect and is so easy to use. Furthermore, it is inexpensive and very easy to make, as it only involves using flour, salt, water and a microwave oven. Allow the children to use their imaginations to create anything from a simple, tall cross to a soldier carrying an injured comrade. In all cases, make sure the children create a base or plinth for their monuments to stand on, having them connected and standing before baking. Once baked, salt dough models do not adhere to most surfaces.

If the models are then gently placed into a plant pot with soil surrounding the base, poppies can be inserted into the soil around remembrance time each year. It may be possible to plant a little rosemary, which is the floral symbol of remembrance.

This is a great activity to involve schools or young people's groups such as Scouts, Girl Guides or Boys and Girls Brigades. If your congregation provides tea and coffee after the Remembrance Service, invite the young people to adorn the tables (where people sit to drink) with their memorials.

10

Advent

'Prepare the way for the Lord, make straight paths for him.'
Matthew 3:3

Introduction

Christmas is coming, the goose is getting fat … you probably know the rest! Yes, Advent (meaning 'arrival') is the four-week period when we look forward to Christmas. It prepares us for the imminent arrival of Jesus and we often think about a theme of getting ready or being prepared. It is also a good opportunity to think of Jesus' second coming and reflect on His instructions to be ever vigilant, as He may come at any time.

In churches across the world, candles are lit on each of the four Sundays that precede Christmas Day, which, for many cultures, is 25 December. Children become increasingly excited and open doors on their advent calendars from 1 December through to Christmas Eve. To add to the excitement, there are even chocolate treats in many of them.

The candles help remind us of Jesus' claim to be the 'Light of the World' and at a time of short days and long, dark nights, this is more easily appreciated than at other times in the year.

Possible themes

- Anticipating.
- Preparing.
- Waiting (patiently).
- Light.

- Hope.
- Angels.
- Prophecies.

So what could we get up to?

The build-up to Christmas is invariably an exciting time and one where people in communities tend to draw together. Despite many of these people not having much particular interest in Jesus or anything to do with church, they will nevertheless usually take part in ecclesiastical activity around this time. It may be due to a feeling of tradition, identifying with Christian culture, or even being aware of a sense of the spiritual significance of the season. Whatever it may be, this is a huge missional opportunity for churches across the country. In Advent, getting co-operation for a project from sections of the community is therefore usually easier.

Light is a theme for Advent, as this beach hut clearly demonstrates.

3D Advent calendars

A few years ago, a church on the south coast of England came up with a brilliant idea of utilising its seaside resort's beach huts for an unusual advent calendar. The huts were owned by a number of individuals and groups, with each owner being invited to put on a display or tableau with a biblical theme for a different evening in December up to Christmas Eve. Some featured lights, angels or stars while others, understandably, featured the stable scene. On each evening, a crowd would gather around a particular hut with the doors opened to reveal an innovative display, carols would be sung and then mince pies (along with fair trade chocolate) served. This is now a well-established event and attracts hundreds of people.

Such an idea can be adapted for the vast majority of congregations that are further inland. A church in the south of England, having been inspired by the beach hut initiative, runs a similar idea around town, using people's garages. Shopkeepers can be invited to provide a window display; creative schools, nurseries and youth groups can display their talents in classrooms, foyers or even in church halls. Furthermore, different groups within a congregation can create their own scenic displays, with perhaps a knitting group producing woolly characters in a stable scene, or a worship group creating a choir of angels from various craft materials.

Waxing lyrical!

Many years ago, a friend of mine in Aberdeenshire kept bees and apart from selling honey, he introduced me to the joys of making candles using sheets of beeswax. Having a soft, sticky and pliable nature, these sheets are easy to manipulate and ideal for creating a variety of styles. Candle-making in the normal sense is perhaps not an activity that is easy to organise, but using beeswax sheets makes it a much cleaner, safer and straightforward undertaking. It is an enjoyable activity to supervise and allows for numerous designs, as different coloured sheets can be cut and overlaid on each other. The sticky character of the wax helps to 'fuse' pieces together. A hair dryer can help fuse pieces better, but it is not essential. Using pieces of string for the wick is not recommended. Rolls of wick are easy to obtain (usually from the same vendors who sell the beeswax) and cost little.

Advent is a time of hope, when we consider Jesus as the Light coming into a dark world, so candles feature prominently. Indeed, images of candles commonly appear on Christmas cards and a good number of candles will be used as decorations, surrounded by holly, silver-painted twigs and poinsettia leaves.

Many schools use church buildings for an end-of-term Christmas service, so if your congregation is one that welcomes the school in this way, why not invite the students to make candles for window displays? Each Sunday during the season, a candle or even a small display of candles may be lit and displayed on a suitable window sill. Alternatively, they could be displayed in an appropriate area at the school, although school term usually ends before the final Sunday, so this will need to be taken into consideration.

This activity can easily be incorporated into the '3D advent calendars' mentioned earlier, as a key element for all kinds of scenes that involve light.

For details on how to create candles from beeswax sheets, see Chapter 14.

11

Christmas

'Do not be afraid. I bring you good news of great joy that will be for all the people. Today in the town of David a Saviour has been born to you, he is Christ the Lord.' Luke 2:10–11

Introduction

Christmas is the most celebrated of Christian festivals, although many of those celebrating will have no personal connection to its spiritual significance. As we know so well, the importance of Jesus' birth is often lost among the jollification. So many people around us will enjoy what, for them, is simply a winter festival, where they may eat and drink to excess, and like us all, exchange lots of presents and cards.

Yet, among all the secularised elements, many people gravitate towards their local churches at Christmas. At my own church in Scotland, attendances at our various Christmas services are much higher than normal and made up of many unfamiliar faces. Whatever the motivation is for people to draw near, this is clearly an opportunity for significant engagement with them.

So what could we get up to?

Card contest

The sending of greetings cards has been a key part of Christmas since the nineteenth century and despite the arrival of email, text and social media, cards are still sent in their millions and then adorn our homes until early January. Handmade cards are on the increase and receiving one that has been especially made for someone is invariably much more appreciated than one that has been 'shop-bought'.

Children love designing Christmas cards, so run a competition!

Children love designing and producing their own cards and a number of companies now work with schools and youth organisations to market the designs to sell cards, tea towels, mugs, etc. It can be quite a thrill, as a child, to observe your design go into print and see family members proudly snap up the merchandise! My own church in central Scotland has, for a good number of years, conducted a competition for local primary school children to design its annual Christmas card. The winning design is then printed on several hundred cards which are given out at Christmas services and events. To add to the kudos of 'mass production', the winning pupil also receives a prize that is awarded at one of the services. It is a simple idea but one that brings a much-needed biblical reminder to children, as the church encourages a Bible-based design. Running such a competition is easy to arrange and apart from choosing who should judge the designs, or what prize to purchase, there is little effort involved – apart from printing out the cards, if it is decided to produce them 'in-house'.

Nativity in a box

The weeks leading up to Christmas are often a time when charitable organisations launch their 'Christmas appeals'. Fundraising initiatives by churches up and down the land help raise vast amounts of money for worthy causes and provide a great witness to Jesus' command to love our neighbours as ourselves. The following activity lends itself well to a fundraising venture.

During a recent Christmas season, a church in Carlisle purchased a large batch of 'matchbox nativities' from a fairtrade organisation. These exquisite novelties from

Peru featured a baby Jesus in a tiny manger, a kneeling Mary and Joseph and two animals – all carved from wood and carefully painted. All were neatly packed into a decorative matchbox. Church members then gave them away to members of the public. While this is an excellent idea, getting your community involved in something similar might be helped if there is also a good cause to raise money for.

If you know talented people (particularly outside the church) who are good at working with wood, clay or who are even experts in origami, why not ask them to create very small characters for a nativity scene, small enough to fit them all in a matchbox? These may then be sold for a charitable cause, while also reminding those receiving them of the real meaning of Christmas.

Matchboxes come in all sorts of sizes these days and so making the figures fit in such a tiny space may not necessarily be such a headache. You could, of course, choose to design and build your own 'matchboxes' out of stiff card. This may make the decorating easier, as you will not have to mask the original cover design as you would for shop-bought boxes, although plain, white matchboxes can be purchased (in bulk) from craft suppliers.

Pocket-sized Christmas gifts like these
are always much appreciated.

Fancy some fun with a flash mob?

One recent Christmas, a church on the west coast of Scotland decided to get together with other local churches to write a song, choreograph a dance for it and then act out a story based on the song for an online video. Furthermore, the song became available on a CD. Three local ministers (Presbyterian, Baptist and Catholic) played the parts of the Wise Men who were seeking a baby born to be a king. Dressed in their regal, middle-eastern costumes, they visited banks, offices, restaurants, a shopping centre and a variety of other places, asking where they may find the king while gently encouraging all kinds of people to join in with their wacky dance. The video is enjoyable to watch and shows a surprising number of people happily shedding their inhibitions and having fun, at the same time being reminded of the biblical Christmas narrative. Such a venture captured the imagination of the community and received very favourable press coverage.

This opens up a raft of ideas, but the very notion of dressing up in biblical costumes and visiting public places would attract attention! People are more prone to join in with all kinds of activities around Christmas, simply because of it being a time for inclusion and merriment. If you have carol singers to add to the occasion, it is very likely that shoppers will pause to sing along, even if they baulk at the thought of dancing. If you 'plant' a number of people from your church within the shoppers to be a 'flash mob' who appear to spontaneously join in with the singing and dancing, it would not take long to gain a substantial crowd. This, of course, is not a new concept, but if well organised and appropriate permission is sought, it can provide a wonderful opportunity to show that the local congregation does have fun and is happy to engage with its community. Furthermore, someone can hand out invitations to Christmas services, while someone else can offer mince pies to increase the sense of hospitality and welcome.

12

Special occasions

Be wise in the way you act towards outsiders; make the most of every opportunity.
Colossians 4:5

Introduction

We have steadily worked our way through the church calendar and yet there are a number of further opportunities for engaging with local communities through the arts. This chapter lists a number of these, along with an artistic idea for each one.

Saints days

Each of the countries within the British Isles has its own patron saint and a designated date to commemorate him. In some areas these dates have, over recent years, become less significant, so in case you may be unaware of them, here they are:

1 March – St David (Wales)
17 March – St Patrick (Ireland)
23 April – St George (England)
30 November – St Andrew (Scotland)

Each saint had a fascinating life story that usually involved an element of legend, but all of them helped spread the Gospel message and remain a source of inspiration. Each of the dates dedicated to them relate to the anniversary of their deaths.

Images immediately spring to mind with all four: leeks for St David, a shamrock for St Patrick, a dragon for St George and the diagonal cross for St Andrew. Why not run a competition in the local school to design a flag for their chosen saint? A special school assembly could be held where members of the congregation can retell stories from his life (and mission) and how he came to be the patron saint (there is plenty of information available online). At the assembly, the winning design can be announced and a suitable prize for the competition, such as an age-appropriate book on the saint, be awarded.

Blessing of the backpacks

In the USA, many congregations support their local schools in a novel way. At the start of the new school year a special service is held in which children's school bags receive a blessing. In these bags will be homework, books, pens, pencils, etc. and all content, including any lunchboxes, will be prayed over for the year ahead. These services also allow for gifts to be given such as pencil cases or, in some cases, new bags. Families on low incomes would be particularly appreciative of these gifts. Each child should hopefully come away having gained a sense of the support of his or her local congregation. The service is beginning to appear in parts of the UK but is still largely unknown among British schoolchildren.

Hosting such a service presents artistic opportunities, for example designing a luggage tag that may be tied onto each bag. On these may be a short Bible verse and the best wishes of the congregation. At the service, these can be awarded to each child. Let's not forget the teachers, too! Why not have another tag designed for staff or create something for their desks such as a paperweight or a desk-tidy?

Country shows

Many rural areas have their own country shows, where farming and agricultural exhibitions occur and a vast range of other attractions take place. Local churches often get involved and provide hospitality. Some shows will even have their own chaplain. Often churches will set out their stall in a tent or marquee. Again, opportunities for some creativity arise. Creating an eye-catching banner to adorn the tent would be an enjoyable pursuit. Admittedly, the banners may not need to be designed each year, but there are further creative opportunities in the form of items that may be given away, for example bookmarks, fridge magnets, badges and key rings. Why not take matters a step further and invite people to come into the tent and make these things? Badges are fun to make and badge-making machines, along with the accessories, are easily available to hire or buy. Furthermore, they are relatively easy to use.

Get involved in whatever is happening!

In early October each year there is a jazz festival in the area where I live. Over the weekend concerned, various pubs and hotels host all manner of jazz acts and a parade takes place on the Sunday. My church realised that this presented an opportunity and it wasn't long before a specified 'Jazz Service' on the Sunday morning became a key part of the festival's programme. The church sanctuary has, ever since, been packed with visitors as hymns old and new are sung to the pacey rhythms of banjos, drums, trumpets and saxophones. One year a visiting musician just wandered in from the street and, with his trombone, simply joined in with 'O when the Saints go marching in'!

Not every area will have a jazz festival, of course, but so many other themed local events take place across our countries. We need to tap into these with some creativity of our own. There are also national events that we could make use of, too. Royal weddings, sporting occasions and anniversaries of significant historic events are all prime examples. We have a Gospel message to proclaim and we are also quite likely to have a lot of artistic talent among us to help proclaim it!

'How to' section

Introduction

Beginners, please!

It is quite likely that much of this section will be familiar to a good number of people. Equally, however, there will be many who will be keen to take on some of the aforementioned artistic activities but may not have attempted them before. This section is geared towards these individuals but, then again, those more accustomed to the activities may find a fresh angle or discover new tools or materials.

Whatever your situation, I trust the following chapters will be of great help and demonstrate that none of the activities need be difficult or too burdensome to consider. Indeed, I sincerely hope you will be greatly encouraged and spurred into action!

13

Banners and timelines

Introduction

In terms of involvement and inclusivity, making banners and timelines are ideal activities to organise. In each case, people can bring a wide range of ideas, skills and experience to each activity. There are, therefore, no fixed methods for creating banners or timelines and much of this chapter should be considered as a guideline.

Banners

Church banners are commonplace in our churches and much of what is written here will most likely be 'old news' to some. Equally, however, there will be many who would like to know how to get started and yet others who may value fresh ideas and tips. So let's begin!

What you will need

Unlike more specific activities, banner making is only limited by one's imagination. You may require little in terms of materials or a vast range of fabrics and adornments. It all depends on the project. Below is a sample list of items, to which many more could be added. However, some of them may not be needed. For example, some banner makers never use needles and thread, but always use a strong craft glue to affix certain fabrics.

- Curtain fabric.

- Felt.
- Old towels.
- Blankets and sheets.
- Ribbon.
- Wool.
- Card or paper (for stencil letters and numbers).
- Scissors.
- Needles and thread.
- Pins.
- Craft glue.
- Fabric pens.
- Curtain rods.
- String, twine or rope cord (for hanging).
- Tape measure.
- Any 'innovative' material such as bubble wrap for water effects.

Some straightforward methods

Before any materials are chosen, it is an obvious requirement to have a design pre-drawn and an estimate of the size of the banner. You will need to include in the design and measurements the means of hanging. A simple method of hanging would involve a curtain pole or rod (cut to size) with finials and a length of cord to wrap around the finials at each end (see figure below).

Hanging banners with curtain poles is both practical and attractive.

To begin, cut out your background from a strong, 'heavy' piece of material. This ensures the banner will hang flat and not easily waft in any draught. Furthermore, it will be able to take the weight of whatever material you attach to it. To help achieve consistency with the size and shape of letters and numbers, cut out stencils from card or strong paper beforehand. So if, for example, you use felt, you may then draw around the stencils onto your felt material and simply cut along the outlines to create your letters and numbers. This will create a more professional appearance to your phrases, Bible quotations, etc. Use strong craft glue, which dries clear, to stick shapes and letters, etc. to your background. As banners are generally viewed from a distance, images and lettering will need to be large and bold with a strong contrast to the colour of the background. Examples of this contrast would be yellow on dark blue, orange on purple or bright green on maroon.

Using cloth fabrics need not be the extent of banner work. All kinds of materials can produce striking effects. For example, quilted material can offer a more '3D' effect and small, coloured wooden beads can give an appearance of berries (see figure).

Fruit can be easily represented on banners by using wooden beads.

Be organised

It is likely that with so many possibilities in respect of material and designs, a good storage facility will be needed. A church in Fife, Scotland has a room designated for banner making, complete with a storage cupboard that houses a tower of stacking boxes. Each box contains different sorts of items. One has press studs, sequins and other small adornments, while another has pieces of felt and yet another contains various ribbons and so forth. A further space is used for all sorts of fabrics and yet another for tools. If you have limited funds, store various small items in used ice cream tubs, label them and stack them.

But remember ...

Once you have hung your banner, do not leave it there for years on end. What at first will appear as a wonderful addition to a worship space or a community hall will, over time, become an unnoticed piece of furniture, risking wear and tear and starting to look 'tired'. Once the relevance for having a banner has passed, it would be wise to take it down. In due course, it may be replaced with another fresh banner that relates to something new.

Timelines

How you construct a timeline is limited only by your imagination and creativity. There is no classic design to them but, as a guide, you will need to think on a big scale and run the chronology from left to right. To help the viewer make sense of it all, it would be wise to have a bold, single coloured line running through the entire design. This is the timeline itself and all events would connect to a part of it. The simplest way of doing this would be to use a long length of strong ribbon. Depending on your choice of background, the ribbon, being lightweight, can be easily attached with staples, craft glue or even hook and loop strips (the most popular brand name for which begins with 'V'!). Along the timeline, at regular intervals you may put key dates. Some designs may use decades or centuries as the key points along the way (see figure below). Once you have a basic idea of how it is to be laid out, it is entirely up to you as to what is exhibited. One striking effect is to pin a string or wool line from the appropriate date to the relevant information and/or artefact (see figure below).

Possible background items

- Portable screens.
- Exhibition boards.
- Curtain.

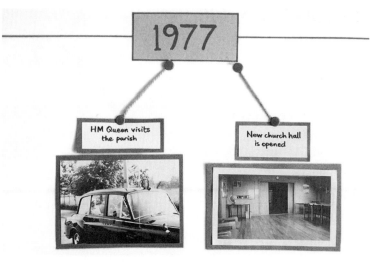

Old photographs always attract interest on timelines.

- Lining paper or wallpaper.
- Sheets.
- Tablecloth.
- Flags and/or banners.

Possible materials and items needed

- Card.
- Paper.
- Marker pens.
- Ribbon.
- Coloured string or wool.
- Scissors.
- Stapler or staple gun.
- Drawing pins.
- Sticky tape.
- Tables.
- Easels.

What to possibly exhibit

- Photographs.
- Paintings and drawings.
- Letters.
- Significant documents or certificates.
- Newspaper articles.
- Maps.
- Architect's drawings.
- Medals, badges, etc.
- Monitor for old movie footage.
- Written information to accompany any of the above.

14

Easy-peasy crafts

Introduction

When it comes to craft activities, there are endless ideas and materials involved. From building a snowman out of plastic cups to painting tiny pebbles, there are limitless artistic projects to embark upon – so much so that this chapter has had to be restricted to those activities mentioned earlier. However, as with so much of this publication, one idea leads to another, so even the few items mentioned here may spark innovative thinking for further activities.

Fridge magnets (from Chapter 1)

Hardly a home in the land is without a fridge or freezer and attached to their doors will be at least a handful of magnetised decorations. Even magnetic 'pins' are now available that can affix paper and card items. Those homes with children often find their fridges and freezers covered with all manner of drawings and artistic pieces of schoolwork.

What you will need

- Drawing/colouring materials.
- Card or thick paper.
- Laminating pouches (usually supplied in A5 and A4 sizes).
- Laminator.
- Roll of adhesive magnetic strip.
- Scissors.

Method

Once you have completed your picture on the paper or card, place it inside a laminating pouch and carefully trim the pouch so that a border of about 5mm surrounds your paper or card. Having switched on a laminator earlier (they often take a few minutes to warm up), gently feed the pouch through the machine. Please be careful as certain parts of the laminator may be very hot. This is definitely a step to be taken by adults, or children under adult supervision.

Once the laminated artwork has cooled down, cut off four small pieces of magnetic tape, peel off the backing and affix the sticky side to the back of your work at the four corners (see figure below). All that remains to be done is to apply to a metallic surface (see figure below) and enjoy!

Using magnetic tape is extremely simple, yet effective.

Fridge magnets are simple to make and act as good reminders.

Egg painting (from Chapter 6)

The art of painting eggs is an ancient one and, with pun intended, I don't want to 'teach granny to suck them' by describing how it can be done! However, let us cover some basics. It is obvious that the eggs will need to be hard-boiled before you begin, otherwise you will run considerable risk of breaking them with a resultant mess and lost artwork.

What you will need

- Hard-boiled eggs.
- Paint (glass paint or fabric paint will give the most vibrant look).
- Paintbrushes.
- Egg cups (to hold the eggs steady).

Method

As mentioned above, how to paint eggs really needs no great description, other than to suggest that you paint either the top half or bottom half first and then place the unpainted section in an egg cup to let the paint dry. Once the paint is dry, simply work on the other half and place the egg in the reverse way to allow for the paint to dry once more.

There is no limit to what you may paint, although an Easter message would be appropriate. Painting faces is fun and you could even paint individual disciples (see figure below).

Eggs are ideally shaped for drawing human heads and faces!

Empty tomb egg cups (from Chapter 6)

Without wishing to advertise any one brand, there are certain confectioners who produce creamy chocolate eggs around Easter. These eggs are individually wrapped in coloured foil and are ideal for giving out as small prizes, gifts, etc. The plastic shot glasses mentioned in Chapter 6 therefore need to be small enough to allow the eggs to 'sit' snugly in. The ideal size of aperture will be between 35mm and 50mm (between 1.5 and 2 inches), depending on the brand of the egg. The capacity of these glasses would be around 40ml. You may want to take a sample egg to the shops and measure 'in situ' to make sure it fits.

What you will need

- Small plastic shot glasses.
- Paint (glass or fabric paint is preferred, but poster paint is inexpensive).
- Black and white (or grey) poster paint.
- Paintbrushes.
- Permanent marker pens (fine point).
- Coloured sticky dots, shapes, etc.

Method

Before you begin, remember that the shot glass will need to be painted in an upside-down position! Using black and white poster paints, mix a grey colour and then completely cover the outside of the 'egg cup'. This will help create a better image of a tomb, while also allowing the detailing to adhere to the surface. In effect, the smooth, shiny nature of the shot glass needs a dull undercoat.

Create the empty opening of the tomb (about the size of a penny) by using a black permanent marker pen or black paint. Draw or paint the large stone that covered the entrance slightly to one side and then draw occasional items of greenery around the rest of the base (which, remember, is the actual top!).

Use whatever material you wish in order to create an Easter message. By having earlier painted the surface in grey, a strong white paint is ideal, but you could use sticky labels or anything you prefer (see figure opposite).

An egg cup to accompany the egg reinforces the Easter message.

Harvest food baskets (from Chapter 8)

There is really no specific way to make these, but if you are completely new to the idea and quite possibly lack experience in basket weaving, then the following method is an ideal way to get started.

What you will need

- A template of a box for cutting out (for photocopying).
- Strong but flexible A4-sized sheets of card.
- Spare card for the carry handles.
- Craft glue.
- Masking tape.
- Scissors.
- Any artistic material for decoration.

Method

Draw your template according to the size and shape you require. As a guide, use a size that will fit onto A4-sized card. This size is most commonly available and in plentiful supply. The template will need to include a base, all four sides and added flaps on either side of the two shorter sides (see figure below). Once drawn, simply photocopy onto as many sheets of card as you need.

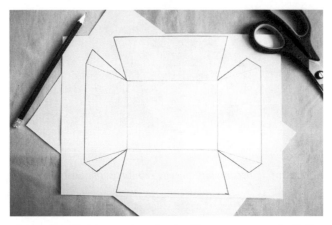

A template that is easy to cut out will encourage productivity.

You then need to cut out the template, making sure you have a decent amount of card left for a carry handle. For this it is recommended you use a strip across the width of the card (about 21cm or 8.25 inches long) and no more than 2.5cm or an inch wide. You can make it wider, but if it gets too wide, those receiving baskets may find it difficult to see the contents!

At this point, you may wish to decorate the basket in any way you choose. Children would particularly enjoy this part of the process and a good addition would be an appropriate harvest message or greeting from the congregation that can be hand-written on the sides.

To construct the cut-out, simply fold along the various lines and glue the flaps to the inside of the longer sides. Craft glue will work well, but glue sticks will suffice, provided not too much weight is placed in the box afterwards. Take the strip you have cut from the leftover card for the handle and glue to the inside of each longer side. To strengthen the joins, place a piece of masking tape over the appropriate area and press down firmly (see figure opposite). Masking tape can be surprisingly strong and this should allow for a decent amount of content without tearing. You may choose to staple the handle, but apart from being unsightly, it is possible for hands or fingers to be scratched on the staples' sharp edges.

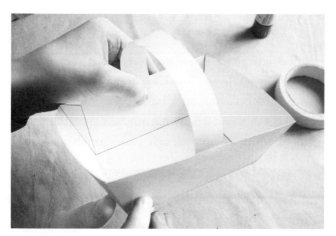

Using masking tape helps make a strong and clean join.

You may need to experiment with different items to gauge the strength of your basket. If it starts to lose its shape, then there's too much weight in it! Grapes are ideal for 'bulking' the load if, for example, only two apples are enough to reach weight capacity.

Beeswax candles (from Chapter 10)

Of all the craft activities I have taken part in, making candles out of beeswax sheets has been by far the most enjoyable. Maybe it is because of the speed at which you can see your creations develop, or the soft pliability of the wax in your fingers, but it is certainly therapeutic and does not require any great level of skill – which is good news for me!

What you will need

- Non-stick baking tray.
- Sheets of beeswax.
- Roll of wick.
- Scissors.
- Sharp knife.
- Ruler.

Method

Before getting started, ensure the beeswax sheets are at room temperature. If they are cold, they may be too brittle and break as soon as you start to roll them.

Place the beeswax sheet on a non-stick baking tray and position a length of wick across one end of the sheet, about 0.5cm in from the edge. Allow the wick to exceed the width of the sheet, about 1.5cm each side (see figure below).

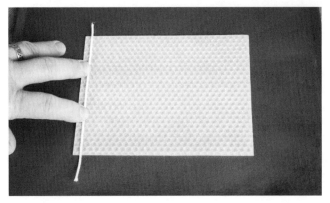

Allow a slight overlap when positioning your wick for a beeswax candle.

To make a straight candle, carefully roll the edge evenly across the wick, making sure it is securely gripped. Keep slowly rolling as tightly as possible, always checking the candle does not 'drift' out of shape (see figure below).

When rolling a beeswax sheet, keep the edges straight and parallel.

When you get to the end, gently press the edge of the sheet into the body of the candle, so the join will be virtually invisible (see figure opposite). Finally, simply snip off the excess wick at the bottom end of the candle and trim the wick at the top to around 1cm.

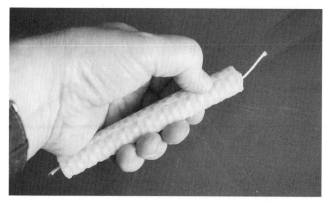

After rolling a beeswax sheet, gently press the end into the candle.

To make a conical candle (looking like a helter-skelter), children will need adult supervision for the cutting. Place a sturdy ruler diagonally across the sheet then, using a sharp knife, carefully cut along the edge of the ruler to create two right-angled triangles (see figure below). Put one triangle to the side and with the other, carry out the same rolling procedure as described above, ensuring that the non-diagonal side is closest to you (see figure on p. 70). When you have finished rolling and pressing in the edge, your candle should have a conical shape (see figure on p. 70). The conical nature of your candle can be varied between being long and slim to short and fat, by simply changing the side of your leading edge for rolling.

Beeswax sheets are soft and easy to cut for conical designs.

Rolling a diagonally cut beeswax sheet requires a bit more care.

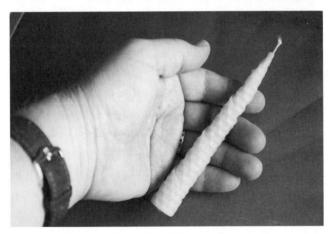

A conical candle is easily produced from a triangular beeswax sheet.

Whichever design you choose, you can easily embellish your candle by cutting regular slits along one edge (for conical candles, the diagonal edge). When you have rolled the candle, pull out 'petals' from your slits and gently fold them out. If you have different coloured sheets, you may overlay two different colours for conical versions and as you roll, one will 'drift' ever so slightly from the other to create a coloured spiral effect.

It may be helpful to take a small scrap of beeswax and wrap it around the base of your wick to help make it easier to light. (Lighting the candle may require a few more seconds than lighting a normal candle on a cake, so ensure it is carried out by an adult or a responsible young person under adult supervision and, if possible, with a long match.)

15

Pancake art

Introduction

Although pancake art is growing in popularity, it is far from easy. As the old saying goes, 'practice makes perfect' and if you can spare some time, with a bit of patience, you can really start to enjoy creating all kinds of images – ones that you can also enjoy eating!

The basic technique involves varying the time you take to cook the pancake, once the pancake mixture hits the hot pan. The key aspect to remember is the longer the cooking, the darker the image. Speed is also vital. You don't want to burn your pancakes, so as soon as you start creating an image, you will need to keep going. If you are too slow, then by the time you've finished your masterpiece, the earliest part of the work will be charred and the smoke alarms may have gone off! The ideal tool to use here is a squeezy sauce bottle, similar to the type you may see in cafes and chip shops. It is usually made of soft plastic, has a slim 'snout' and an attached cap to cover the nozzle when not in use. Empty washing-up liquid bottles can be used, but they need endless rinsing once empty and always carry the risk of giving a soapy taste to your pancakes!

Needless to say, this activity is suitable for adults and responsible, older children under adult supervision. Younger children can still be involved by drawing designs to be cooked or, as mentioned in Chapter 3, decorating pancakes that have cooled down.

What you will need

- Pancake mix (ready to pour).
- Knob of butter or margarine.
- A hob to cook on.
- Frying pan.
- Squeezy bottle with slim 'snout'.
- Spatula.
- Plates to place cooked pancakes on.
- Illustrations you may wish to copy from.

Method

Before cooking the pancakes, ensure your pancake mix is runny enough to come through the nozzle of the bottle without any difficulty. If it is too thick, the nozzle will easily clog up and pouring will soon become difficult, causing much frustration and ruined artwork.

Once you have everything you need neatly laid out, pour your pancake mix into the squeezy bottle. Ensure you have a generous amount in the bottle because when the pouring starts, you will not have time to refill. Alternatively, have a number of bottles filled up and at hand so you can quickly switch to a fresh bottle.

Drop a knob of butter or margarine into your frying pan and heat the pan. Swirl the butter around the pan as it melts and once it has completely melted, your cooking surface should be sufficiently 'lubricated'. Now you are ready to squeeze out your initial artwork.

Let us pretend you wish to create an image of a face. You may have a simple drawing at hand to copy from. Make a note of the darker areas in the drawing such as hair, eyes, lips, any shadow from the nose, etc. These are the features to 'draw' by carefully squeezing out the mixture onto the pan (see figure opposite). Keep the pan steady at this stage, as all your artwork is disconnected and each piece will need to stay in position for the next step.

Allow for the various pieces to solidify and then wait a few more seconds before 'filling in' the rest of the face (and adding ears), thereby joining everything together and creating, at this point, an indiscernible image. However, the really exciting bit is now upon us!

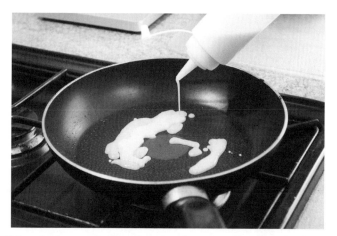

With pancake art, the first drops on the pan will end up the darkest.

Once the entire pancake has solidified, gently turn over the pancake with a spatula and you should see an image of a face. Carefully lift it off the pan and place on a plate to cool down. Do not despair if it looks a mess! Keep practising, varying the cooking times between different shades. If nothing else, you can always enjoy eating all the earlier aborted attempts!

Other ideas

Apart from the technique described, you can always squeeze out different shapes to create letters, numbers, heart shapes and so on. Furthermore, by creating various sizes of conventional, circular pancakes, you may wish to build up an image. For example, a caterpillar could be made up of varying circular shapes, laid on top of one another, with the smallest pancake at one end and the largest (the head) at the other. Simply add two slim strips of pancake for the antennae and two sultanas for the eyes. Pieces can be fixed together with jam, cream, soft icing, or even chocolate spread.

Using fruit items and cake decorations will allow for all sorts of creativity. Two slices of a strawberry often look very effective as ears for teddy bears or cats. Blueberries usually make good eyes and grapes can sometimes look good as noses.

Using food colouring opens up a whole new range of artistic possibilities, but perhaps that is best left to a later time when you have already mastered the basic techniques.

16

Paint, pastels and palettes

Whether we are drawing, painting or colouring, we rarely have to look far for a pencil or a cheap set of felt-tip pens. There is much more material available of course and so for those unfamiliar with artistic media and materials, here's a quick guide to the most popular means of creating visual masterpieces.

It would be wise to work in one medium for a while, simply playing and experimenting. All media take time to be fully grasped and to produce anything satisfying.

Drawing

Pencils are the principal tools here. It's important to know that the conventional graphite pencils have grades of hardness and softness. The softer the graphite, the easier it is to shade and to create levels of light and dark. Most pencils are graded 'HB', which is neither hard nor soft. For hardness, we go to 'H' then '2H', '3H' and so on. The simple rule here is the higher the number, the harder the graphite. These pencils are often used in mathematical drawings, but artistically they are not suitable. The 'B' graded pencils are of much more use to us here. Again, the rule is the higher the number (e.g. '4B'), the softer the graphite. Beware, however, as softer pencils produce images that are more easily smudged. If you are not careful, your pictures can look dreadfully grubby!

Pencil crayons are a safe, no fuss, clean option and often come in packs that provide a vast range of colours. Some upmarket brands can also be used as water-colours, by dipping them into water. The advantage of all pencil crayons is their ease of use, but their centres can be brittle and, if used roughly, they will easily break.

Charcoal is an exciting medium that, because of its sheer darkness, will offer stark contrasts and will feel almost like painting. However, as with very soft pencils, it can smudge far too easily. Unless it is used very carefully, it can make quite a mess, but that is what makes it fun! Such smudging means it can be easily manipulated. Both pencil and charcoal can also be rubbed out to various degrees, adding to the tone.

Chalk is an inexpensive medium and is easier to use than charcoal, as it can be washed out of most things. We may automatically think of chalk as white, but it is easily available in a vast range of colours. Unlike charcoal and pencil, it should be used on a surface with a slightly rough texture such as cartridge paper or stone.

Pastels

Soft pastels can be great fun, but as with charcoal and very soft pencils, they are chalky, smudge easily and can deposit dust. Smudging can be intentional though, as artists can use them to blend colours and soften images. A gentle swirl with a finger can produce a clever, 'foggy' or hazy effect. For best results, try to use coloured, rough-textured paper that is specifically designed for pastel use. Ordinary white paper is a no-no here.

Oil-based pastels are cleaner to use and, as with their soft counterparts, come in a vast range of colours. Again, they are best used on coloured paper, but whereas they don't particularly smudge, they don't blend so easily. They have a similar feel to wax crayons and create a glossy finish but deliver a clearer, more consistent image, unlike the stippled effect of crayons.

Conte crayons are a 'happy medium' (pun intended!) between soft and oil pastels. They offer a pleasant tone and tend to come in a range of natural browns and reds, along with black and white (ideal for highlighting). They are available both as short 'sticks' and as pencils. The pencils are cleaner to use but less suited to broad strokes and shading of large areas. Artists like to use Conte crayons for figure drawing and portraits, but they are also very useful for the initial sketch of a pastel drawing, as the colours mix easily.

Painting

Oil paints are wonderful to use. The colours mix well and as the paint takes a long time to dry, compositions can be re-worked again and again. A major concern can, of course, be the potential for the paint to end up where it shouldn't! Soap and water will have limited effect on stains. A bottle of turpentine substitute or white spirit will be needed – not just for cleaning a mess or rinsing brushes but also to help 'thin' the paints and allow for more variation in shading and mixing. The trouble with these thinning agents is that they do tend to emit a strong odour and so some considerable ventilation is advised.

A palette is useful for mixing the paints and for practising brush strokes. If palettes are not easily available, then any old pieces of dry, smooth wood should suffice. Canvas is the ideal surface for oil paints. These days, it is rare for artists to stretch their own canvas and canvas boards are widely available in a range of sizes. The smaller sizes are surprisingly inexpensive and can be found in bargain outlets.

Acrylic paints are water-based and so are much easier to clean, thereby removing the need for smelly cleaning/thinning agents. Like oils, they come in small 'toothpaste' style tubes and broadly offer the same range of colours. They have the same texture as oils but dry a lot quicker (a few hours, rather than a day or so, depending on the temperature). This can be advantageous for those who prefer to work quickly, but there are others who like their options for adjusting and correcting their work left open for as long as possible and so tend to prefer using oil-based paints.

As with oils, a palette and a canvas surface are recommended. Both types of paint use the same brushes, which have short hairs, often arranged in a chisel-like shape. This is because they need to be stronger to apply thicker paint.

Watercolours are very popular and, again, need no smelly thinning agent. As they dry fairly quickly, mixing colours has to be a swift affair but, with care, layering different colours on top of each other can create pleasing results. The range of colours is huge and if you can get a white metallic lid on a set of paints, you will be able to mix the colours on it before applying. Brushes for watercolours are soft and pointed. They are not expensive and, as with canvas boards, can be bought at various bargain outlets.

White cartridge paper is the ideal surface for watercolours. Cheap paper will wrinkle due to the moisture, but the thicker cartridge paper absorbs the moisture and stays flat. Invariably, this kind of paper will come in the form of a spiral-bound sketchbook.

Finally, there is no rule on how you mix media. Don't be afraid to try mixing pencil crayon with pastels or pencil with charcoal. The main exception is mixing oil and acrylic paints, while they are still wet!

17

Graffiti art

Introduction

Due to the 'vandalism' of much graffiti we may see on walls, railway embankments, subway tunnels and so on, the whole genre of graffiti art is often considered fairly subversive. Such consideration makes this art form attractive to teenagers and young adults. One of my teenage sons likes it because he says, 'it's edgy'! Used appropriately though, it can be a visually impressive way to convey a message or feeling. Stencil-type graffiti, with some careful planning, enables participants to be confident of good, eye-catching results, without the fear of having to rely on any great drawing ability. This is important in terms of self-esteem, as many participants can feel a sense of achievement – by creating artwork, perhaps for the first time, but also by being able to express themselves through the medium.

This chapter deals not only with how to create graffiti artwork, but also how to help a group of people do likewise. Although there is much preparation involved and many tools and materials required, the rewards can be considerable. A previous colleague of mine has run numerous graffiti workshops and all have proved immensely popular, as well as producing some striking and impressive artwork.

What you will need

For preparing the stencils beforehand

- Images for stencils.
- Laminator and laminating pouches.
- Craft knife.
- Cutting mat.

For designing graffiti

- A3-sized sheets of paper.
- Half-sized paper versions of all the stencils (enough for each person).
- Scissors.
- Glue sticks.

For graffiti

- A well-ventilated or outside venue.
- Spray paints (matt black is best).
- Hardboard, cut into 60cm squares (large DIY stores will cut these for you).
- Emulsion paint in a variety of colours.
- Paint rollers and trays.
- Stencils.

You will also need

- Latex gloves (advisable).
- Dust masks (essential).
- Large tarpaulin or ground sheet.
- Cable ties.
- Drill with 10mm drill bit.
- Hammer and nails.
- Washing line and pegs.
- Talcum powder.

Preparing stencils for the workshop

To make stencils, choose any images, numbers and words you may wish to print onto regular paper. Bearing in mind this will use up a lot of printer ink, print out your letters and numbers as outlines, rather than solid black. Any images need to be converted into pure black and white, using programs such as Microsoft Word and using the picture format options. At this point, make several half-sized copies of all your printouts (enough for each person). You will then need to laminate all your full-sized printed sheets of paper in order to protect them, as well as to help make them durable, so that they can be used several times.

The next stage is time-consuming but worth it! Once completed, this part of the process will save you a lot of preparation time for future activity. You will need to carefully cut out all your laminated images, letters and numbers, using a sharp craft knife, ideally on top of a cutting mat, although a thick piece of cardboard will suffice. Cut out the black parts of your images, but ensure that the overall shape is joined up (see figure below). It is a common mistake to cut out pieces and then find an entire section simply falls out! You will notice this with stencilled numbers and letters. So if, for example, you cut out a number 'zero', you will need a small line above and below the inner circle connecting to the outer circle.

When cutting a graffiti art stencil, ensure it remains 'joined up'!

Preparing boards for the workshop

First, drill holes in the corners of all the hardboards using a 10mm drill bit, 2cm from the corners. The holes allow the boards to be connected together at the end of the workshop. Give each board a coat of emulsion paint, preferably using light or mid-tone colours (not too light or dark), as these work best as a contrast to the black spray paint. At the end of the workshop, you can then assemble the boards into a complete wall with cable ties. Making a wall this way means an equal 'share' in the final display and also allows people to take their own piece of work home with them after the project is over.

Running the workshop

Adult supervision is vital for running this kind of activity and as safety is paramount, there are precautions to make before getting started. Good ventilation is essential so if possible, conduct the workshop outdoors. If this is not possible, or the weather is poor, use a room that is spacious and very well ventilated. Furthermore, ensure there is a good supply of dust masks and possibly latex gloves and some protective clothing. It would also be wise for those taking part to come along in old clothes that they don't mind getting paint on. As spray paints are going to be used, there will be considerable fumes and quite likely a lot of mess (see figure below)! If not working on grass, ensure a tarpaulin or ground sheet is in place to protect the floor surface.

For graffiti art, face masks are essential.

If possible, have examples of graffiti art prepared in advance. It would be sensible to try out your stencils beforehand anyway. You can then show the 'prototypes' to people so that, everyone can see and understand what it is they are trying to create before getting started.

Once everyone has seen the examples and made aware of safety issues, give each participant a sheet of A3 paper (ordinary photocopy paper is ideal) which needs cutting down from a rectangle to a square 30cm by 30cm. This will be half the size of the hardboards. Using the half-sized printouts of all the stencils, people can then create their own designs by cutting them out and arranging them on their A3 sheets, before sticking them down with glue sticks. As workshop leader, you should ensure all participants can be helped to consider various design possibilities.

The spray painting is, of course, the exciting bit! Make sure the spray cans are shaken well before each participant begins and that he or she is wearing a dust mask. The spray painting should be done from a height of about 20cm and at a 45-degree angle (see figure below). Use scraps of paper to mask off areas on the hardboards that are not to be sprayed.

Spraying paint is best done from a height of around 20cm.

When everyone has used the spray paints and completed their artwork, the boards can be joined together and displayed as a 'wall'. This is done by using nails for the top boards and attaching other boards below with the cable ties threaded through the pre-drilled holes (see figure on p. 82).

Hanging graffiti art boards together creates an impressive 'wall'.

The stencils will need to be completely dry before being collected up. A washing line and clothes pegs are ideal for this. When they are dried, lightly 'dust' them with talcum powder, as this will help prevent them from sticking together when they are stacked away.

18

Drama made easy – honest!

Introduction

Everybody enjoys a good drama sketch. Some congregations may be blessed with a dedicated team of budding actors, have access to costumes, props and, of course, good scripts. However, many struggle to find anyone willing to perform and may lack any resources of a theatrical nature.

No worries! A punchy but short sketch that highlights a teaching point is often an effective missional tool and just as with music and dance, it can be a welcome addition to our worship. It need not, however, be an arduous task to put something together and there are some simple ways to perform drama without the need for either great theatrical talent or much preparation.

What about bigger productions such as passion plays?

Most of this chapter concerns short sketches, but a lot of the advice can relate to bigger and lengthier productions. The key difference with large scale drama is that you need to break it down into bite-sized chunks. Try to avoid casting parts that will involve actors having to appear in numerous scenes and needing them to learn vast amounts of dialogue. Passion plays are ideal examples, as apart from the role of Jesus (who needs little dialogue), different characters appear in different scenes.

Unlike short sketches you will, of course, need highly skilled people to direct or produce and, crucially, to co-ordinate matters. Organisational skills will need to be a prerequisite of such people.

Variable venues

Performing a drama sketch need not be the preserve of a church service. There are opportunities for including a small 'skit' in all sorts of ways:

- Models of Café Church are gaining popularity and in instances of specific café events, where some sort of 'up front' leading is taking place, a simple sketch, monologue or dramatic Bible reading can be very effective.
- *Messy Church* is enjoying massive growth across the UK and part of a typical *Messy Church* programme is the Bible story. Dramatising the story can help make its message very powerful and some churches are already doing this.
- More informal get-togethers such as special breakfasts, midweek services and various church social group meetings provide occasions for inviting newcomers and if a good piece of drama is included in the proceedings, then again, this can have a powerful impact on the programme.
- Children and young people are far less inhibited than adults in their behaviour and adding drama to school assemblies or to Youth Group teaching, often using youngsters themselves, is fun and makes the message more memorable (even if performed badly!).

Short and sharp

Drama sketches are, by nature, short. There have been occasions when they have been known to drag on to become mini plays! If a sketch is required for a church service, then a long, drawn-out mega-production is going to seriously lengthen proceedings and unless performed brilliantly, will soon begin to irritate people. If that happens, its purpose may be lost and it will be remembered for all the wrong reasons.

Sketches are usually performed in under three or four minutes. Any longer than this and you may be labouring the intended point. Three or four minutes may seem almost too short, but you would be surprised how much dialogue or action you can put into as little as ninety seconds. If children are in your audience, then because of their shorter attention span, this is particularly important.

Is learning lines a barrier?

Well it need not be! Painstakingly learning your lines so you don't have to carry scripts about or bring things to a shuddering halt when you cannot think of the next line (and panic!) need not be an issue. There are ways to perform a short sketch that avoid any such trauma:

Mime to a narrated script. One person can simply read out a short scenario, while actors mime appropriately. Even the mime can be stylised to keep it simple. This way, the actors take their cues from the narrator, even if they forget the next 'action'. This often works well with Bible stories and the parables of Jesus. Sometimes a short piece of music may suffice and no words need be said. If done well, this can be very powerful.

You can use scripts unashamedly! Sometimes the words are the most important aspect of a piece of drama. In these instances, simply line up the readers and deliver the lines in 'quick-fire' succession. Alternatively, place the readers within the audience who then stand up wherever they are to read out their respective lines.

Cheat! Actors' lines may be written on props and bits of scenery, so they could read them without the audience noticing. Lines could be written inside a newspaper, on the back of a chair, inside a cup – you get the idea.

Cannot think of any actors in your congregation?

It is most likely that we won't have professional actors in our congregations (if we do, then let's make sure we use them!), yet there are always those who enjoy performing a fun sketch or at least are willing to read the Bible lessons. Keeping matters simple allows for all sorts of people to be involved. We are not seeking to perform Shakespeare or Chekov and we certainly want to keep lines to a minimum. If it is a mime that is required, then most people will have a reasonable ability to make gestures or pull facial expressions. All you then need is someone with a good voice or who is a regular Bible reader to narrate.

If your human resources are really stretched, then performing a monologue or reciting a short story (or poem) needs only one person and can still be highly effective.

A mock interview allows for improvisation and only needs two actors. One may have a clipboard with the relevant questions to ask and the interviewee could be a Bible character who simply responds 'in character' (as long as the actor is familiar with the character and any related Bible story, so he or she can answer the questions comfortably). Some simple costume can be worn to add to the effect.

What material?

It would be almost impossible to list all the Christian drama sketches that are available either in shops or online, so I will simply list some tips for writing your own, which is not as arduous as it seems and avoids any copyright or performance rights costs. Besides, if you are writing for an audience you are familiar with, you can easily include 'in jokes' and if you are also familiar with the actors, you can tailor certain parts to suit them ('typecast').

When writing your own material, try to think of the following:

Avoid a cast of thousands. A sketch that involves two or three people can help to keep it brief. Getting numerous actors in and out of positions and making entrances and exits can greatly increase the timescale.

Don't worry about elaborate scenery. If the sketch is to be short (possibly even impromptu), moving items of scenery in and out of position simply adds time and might even take longer than the sketch itself! That said, tables and chairs can easily be included and in a church service, may be positioned during a preceding song or hymn.

Try to include some humour. Whatever the material, even something that conveys a serious message, there should be a funny line or moment that 'warms' the audience to the sketch and draws more attention. Make sure, though, that the humour is not too close to the end of the piece, so that the seriousness of any point becomes compromised.

Begin and end the piece well! A good start that includes a funny line or a very dramatic piece of action will quickly gain attention. A punchline of some sort is a simple but effective way to end your sketch. Alternatively, have a narrator deliver a Bible text that highlights the point you wish to make.

Decide how you are going to make it clear the sketch is over. Without a curtain or a blackout of stage lights, it can often be a problem to convey to people that the sketch has finished (and if they wish, to applaud!). A 'freeze' for a few moments, followed by the actors calmly walking off stage is one method. Alternatively, a short 'bum-bum' from a percussionist or a musical 'ta-dah' is another method, often used in sketches on television.

Keep an eye on the time. When you are writing either dialogue or a narration, keep reading it out loud, while checking your watch or a clock. Bear in mind that often, the shorter and simpler the sketch, the deeper the impact. Furthermore, a shorter sketch means fewer lines to remember and fewer things to go wrong!

Be aware of induction loops. If your sketch is to be in a church service and the sanctuary has an induction loop, then using microphones is preferable. Again, having fewer characters is helpful, as you'll need fewer microphones. It is unwise to have some actors use microphones and others not (unless they do not speak), because those members of the congregation with hearing aids will have their ear pieces set to the loop and will mainly hear from the microphones.

Conclusion

As always, remember that old adage, 'KISS' – 'Keep it simple, stupid!' Simplicity is the key. Try to avoid attempting to get across more than one message and keep the sketch brief. You may discover that by ensuring drama scripts are kept short, you can increase the overall output. So, for example, a series of quick sketches (or 'episodes') staged throughout Advent or Lent may be more effective than a single lengthier one, performed on just one occasion. As in many cases, 'less is more'. Finally, have fun with your writing and performing. When an audience senses you are enjoying it, *they* will start to enjoy it too, no matter how cheesy or corny it may be!

19

Video – helping to avoid an amateurish look!

Introduction

Up until the 1980s, unless you could afford cine equipment, making home movies was a hobby for only a few hardy enthusiasts. Indeed, many towns and villages had a local cine club where skills and resources could be pooled and costs shared to produce all manner of film productions.

Then video recorders arrived in our shops and before long, video cameras (soon to be called 'camcorders') joined them. Due to the low cost of video cassette tape compared to cine film (as well as videotape being able to record sound, as opposed to being a luxury 'extra' for cine), weddings, graduation ceremonies and all sorts of social occasions became easy to record. At the turn of the century, new technology meant we could even record images digitally, thus removing the need for video tape cassettes and, in time, cameras gradually shrank to virtually the size of a fist.

Today, most of us do not use video cassettes at all and images can be recorded on smartphones and tablets. While this opens up so many opportunities for all of us, a good number of people have no particular skills in filming or editing. As a result, if someone who is used to recording a brief moment at a party is then asked to put a short promotional video together, the results can often be very disappointing (or hilarious, depending on your point of view!). Thankfully, many devices have rudimentary editing software and these can help tidy up a good number of movie projects. However, 'prevention is better than cure' and in this chapter we will deal with good practice when filming, in order to save a lot of time during the editing stage. So here are some simple tips to make your productions look far more professional.

Plan ahead

It seems obvious, yet many people run out to film something without thinking through film sequences or camera angles. It is wise to compile a 'storyboard' first. This is a set of drawings in the style of a cartoon strip. The drawings are laid down in the order they should appear on screen and may include close-ups, wide angles, etc. This will help you to be a little more creative and will save you time having to think about how you will film when on location.

Check your light source

Video images look sharper and less 'grainy' if there is plenty of light on the subject. However, some people make the mistake of filming on a bright sunny day and promptly film their subject against the light. Most devices will adjust themselves to take in less light if the image is generally bright but will, as a result, also make the subject appear as a virtual silhouette. However, if you – correctly – have the light source coming from behind the camera, be careful of shadows. Occasionally, I have watched clips where the shadow of the camera and of the person holding it can be seen creeping into the shot!

If lighting equipment is unavailable for indoor filming, try reflecting light with a large sheet of white card, paper or even a sheet of tin foil (avoid touching any foil during filming because it can be a noisy material) to brighten up your subject.

Avoid 'jump cuts'

A common mistake when filming is to shoot a prolonged sequence but restart the recording during it. Allow me to explain. Let us pretend you are filming guests arriving for a wedding at a church. Here come Mr and Mrs Smith, walking up the path and they are taking their time. You film them for a few seconds and then stop to relax. You then lift up your device and film them arriving at the doorway. When you watch back the continuous footage, they will appear to 'jump' nearer the door quite suddenly! To counter this, you need to film what is known as a 'cutaway' shot. In this instance, it could be a quick shot of someone at the door waving to the Smiths. When you cut back to them arriving, the eye will accept the passage of time being shortened on the finished piece of footage. This process is simply 'editing in camera' and saves a possible headache when editing your video footage afterwards.

Check continuity

Continuity is always a problem for even the very best of professional movie directors. As soon as cameras stop filming in the middle of a sequence, anything can change such as the wind blowing an actor's hairstyle the wrong way, the weather getting better or worse, or the actor inadvertently putting a prop in his or her other hand! When the filming restarts, a number of errors may appear in the completed sequence. With video (as opposed to film), it is easy to quickly check back on a recording and note everything that needs to stay the same before shooting the next part of the sequence.

Position the subject correctly

Interviewing a subject sounds straightforward but it needs considerable care. Firstly, a tripod or a very steady hand is required, particularly if the subject is simply sitting or standing. If they are talking to an interviewer, do not position their head in the centre of the frame. Ensure there is virtually nothing between the head and the top of the picture, so that we see more of the subject and less of the empty space above. Depending on where the interviewer is, position the subject slightly to the left or right of the centre. Therefore, if the subject is looking towards the left of the frame, position the camera so that they are slightly to the right in the picture.

Check the background

A classic photographic mistake is one where the photographer is so focused on the subject that they become oblivious of what is behind. The result is often a lamppost or street sign appearing to grow out of the subject's head or, worse still, another person appears to be giving a rude gesture! The same goes for video, only you will also need to check for background noises. The golden rule is to ensure that whatever is in the background is not of more interest than the subject in the foreground.

Use external microphones if possible

Sometimes people have been interviewed in the street and the noise of traffic and people walking past has virtually drowned out the voice of the subject. This can be mitigated by fitting a clip-on microphone to the interviewee, or pointing a microphone towards his or her mouth. Most if not all video cameras and devices have a small socket for external microphones and it is strongly suggested you use them, even indoors. Bear in mind that any fumbling noises on the camera or device will be picked up by the internal microphone, as well as any heavy breathing or sighing by the person filming!

Edit ruthlessly!

Apart from important words spoken by your subject, keep all other shots brief. A good way of learning this technique is to watch TV commercials. They constantly change the picture within a relatively short sequence of thirty or forty seconds, yet still manage to tell a story. Similarly, a few seconds is all you need to show a particular piece of film. Let us go back to Mr and Mrs Smith arriving for the wedding. You need not film them taking more than two or three steps towards the church before you cut to someone waving at the doorway. The wave needs to be less than two seconds before you cut back to the Smiths arriving at the door and greeting the person who waved. If the sequence just described lasts for more than six or seven seconds, it is probably too long! In the professional world, you would be surprised at how much filmed 'footage' does not end up being shown at all.

20

Where to from here?

Always be prepared to give an answer to everyone who asks you to give the reason for the hope that you have.
1 Peter 3:15

Art knows no bounds

Throughout this book we have concerned our artistic projects with special occasions and festivals. Many creative ventures can, of course, be undertaken any time. A considerable number of congregations and church groups operate artistic activities that connect with their local communities all year round. These may involve fundraising for a good cause, operating as a source of therapy, or simply providing enjoyment and self-expression.

It would be encouraging if, after running a project to tie in with one of the key church calendar events, there was some impetus to follow it up with something more regular, or at the very least for it to become an annual occasion. One-off projects are fine, but keeping regular contact with your community's creative people is surely better. More contact allows for relationships to be developed and as the conversations grow, so do the opportunities for us to share our faith.

The long and the short

Christian 'seasons' such as Lent and Advent lend themselves well to a longer-term project, while others such as Harvest are more suitable for a one-day or weekend venture. Whatever the length of your artistic undertaking, it is of course the contact that is so important. Spending quality time with individuals is such a vital factor. Yes, we want to have a successful project, yes, we want everyone to have a rewarding experience and yes, we want to generate goodwill. However, if that is the extent of our objectives, our congregations and church groups will not see any real, lasting growth and any Christian message, while being given an artistic 'boost', may not be so effectively proclaimed.

The events of the ecclesiastical calendar provide touching points with our local communities. Many 'unchurched' people are more receptive to church activity at these times and that is very much at the heart of what this book is about. Doors of opportunity will open and we must be ready to take advantage.

Sharing our faith need not be difficult

In the course of my work, I have discovered again and again that congregations and church groups are very good at engaging with their local communities and regularly provide excellent hospitality. Furthermore, their charitable work and championing of social justice is prodigious and many are held, quite rightly, in high regard by their local communities.

On the other hand, the 'Achilles heel' is a reluctance by the members of these congregations and church groups to talk about their faith or discuss spiritual matters. Indeed, there is a certain aversion to talk about these things with each other!

There is no need to delve into all the many reasons why this is, but if we are to obey Jesus' teaching to 'go and make disciples', we have to open our mouths at some point! There are many ways we can engage with our communities and this book offers a number of them to be considered. They should, in theory, invite enquiry on faith issues and then we can add the 'talk' to the 'walk'! In short, we should be ready for follow-up.

Let us assume you are seated next to a complete stranger, while decorating pancakes (see Chapters 3 and 15). Inevitably, one of you will initiate some small talk. Gradually, you build the conversation and then the stranger says, 'So, are you a member of this church?' You reply that you are and maybe the conversation drifts towards church practice. This often happens and we can easily 'hide' behind church things and not actually mention Jesus at all. However, at this point and without forcing matters, you need to be a little courageous, offer up a very quick, silent prayer and talk about how the church (or the event you are celebrating) has helped your faith. Talking about our faith need not involve having a great biblical knowledge.

Our own personal stories mean much more to a listener than expounding doctrine or quoting lots of scripture. Who knows where the conversation may go from here? It is unlikely that the stranger is going to laugh at you or deride your beliefs. This is because he or she has already joined you to partake in an activity related to a Christian celebration and so, in a sense, is present on your terms. Implicitly, permission is given for you to raise any spiritual matter. The stranger can easily refuse to discuss things further and that is fine. It would be better for that to happen than the stranger wanting to explore Christianity and you never mention it.

Be prepared

On a practical note, it would be wise to have some kind of structure that allows for those who may want to know more. Numerous courses are available that explore the Christian faith and encourage relevant conversation. You may already have the skills and resources within your congregation or church group to devise your own course. Some congregations operate specific home groups for 'beginners'. You will need to prayerfully consider a long-term strategy that is right for you. Whatever you decide, keep matters informal and provide some food. Furthermore, keep up the artistic activity! As people explore faith and discover more about Jesus, why not allow them to express themselves through the arts? It could be through graffiti art, through crafts, through poetry, or through anything!

To summarise, be prepared to follow up on any venture you take on. Longer-term contact increases the opportunity for faith-sharing as well as developing further artistic ideas.

May God bless you and bless all your projects.